INCIDENT INTO EVIL

INCIDENT INTO EVIDENCE
Operational Police Skills

· ·

Trevor Colman

Detective Inspector

McGRAW-HILL BOOK COMPANY

London · New York · St Louis · San Francisco · Auckland · Bogotá
Guatemala · Hamburg · Lisbon · Madrid · Mexico · Montreal
New Delhi · Panama · Paris · San Juan · São Paulo · Singapore
Sydney · Tokyo · Toronto

This book is dedicated to all operational police officers and, in particular, to ex-Superintendent Brian John McCreery and the late Police Sergeant Anthony French who, in their very differing ways, were the inspiration for it being written.

Published by
McGRAW-HILL Book Company (UK) Limited
MAIDENHEAD · BERKSHIRE · ENGLAND

British Library Cataloguing in Publication Data
Colman, Trevor
   Incident into evidence: operational
   police skills.
   1. Great Britain. Police. Duties — Manuals
   I. Title
363.2'2'0941
ISBN 0—07—707088—7

123 MAT 898

Typeset by Hybert · Design & Type, Maidenhead, Berkshire
and printed and bound at the University Press, Cambridge

Contents

Acknowledgements

Acknowledgement and thanks to Alan Walker, Roger Thomas, Gordon Smith, John Shaw, Tom Whitmore and, of course, Angela who all, to a greater or lesser extent, helped.

Part 1

Operational police skills: the system

1 Introduction

This book is concerned with operational police work. It is designed to show how an operational police officer can, by using a systematic approach to an incident, successfully deal with that incident and, equally importantly, present it later in an acceptable documented form.

Although one accepts that there is no substitute for solid practical experience, there are many skills in police work still untaught which, if taught, would greatly assist the rawest recruit.

I am referring to those skills exhibited by some officers which enable them to act in an apparently cool and efficient manner and, more to the point, successfully cope not only with the incident itself but also with all the attendant paperwork, administrative minutiae and court requirements.

There is no secret as to the manner in which such officers perform. They merely *work to a system.*

In introducing this 'new' subject of police skills to readers I am aware that they, the readers, are predominantly police officers and, as such, are wary, sometimes justifiably, of supposedly new ideas.

Let me state from the outset that there is nothing new being taught in this book, for it is based totally on established practical methods and procedures and much, if not all, of the teaching will be familiar to most efficient officers.

What is new, however, is the fact that it is being taught at all and that for the very first time a system of police skills has been codified and set down for all to use.

Operational police skills

The responsibilities of an operational officer

A dictionary definition of the word 'skill' describes it variously as 'expertness, practical mastery' or 'familiar knowledge combined with dexterity'. How then to identify and define police skills?

In order to answer that question one must ask what, in practical terms, is the main purpose of an operational police officer, be he foot patrol, mobile or criminal investigation department?

I would suggest that it is initially to deal with incidents which he attends and then to convert those incidents into such a form that a decision can be made as to the participants in those incidents.

In other words the operational officer has *two main responsibilities*. These are:

The two
responsibilities

Maintain
the peace

Statement
report

1. To maintain or restore the peace at the scene of an incident.
2. To present that incident in an acceptable form (statement/report/file) to a decision maker.

Working to a system

Many officers are extremely proficient at discharging the first responsibility and find great satisfaction in so doing. They are described as 'good on the street' or 'practical bobbies' and they come to look upon themselves as just that.

Very few of these officers, however, do themselves justice when they tackle the second and equally important responsibility. Often their supervisors talk of them as 'poor on paper', 'needs assistance with reports' or 'OK arresting people but needs someone else to sort it out'.

Very quickly, because they have problems with this second responsibility, many young officers wrongly come to the conclusion that they cannot and never will master this second phase of police work. Both they and those to whom they submit their work believe it is their lack of skill in the compilation of paperwork that is the root cause of the problem. Nothing could be further from the truth. *The real problem occurs at the very first instant the officers arrive at the scene of an incident.*

Because the less than efficient officer does not work to a system, he immediately begins to make mistakes, usually of omission, which are later reflected in the poor presentation of a file or report.

In other words the later problems are caused by the inability, *at the time of dealing with an incident*, to work in such a manner (or to a system) so that the two main responsibilities of the operational officer can be met.

This, more often than not, results in the debilitating task of re-interviewing witnesses and sometimes suspects, the taking of further or additional statements, the frantic search for overlooked pieces of evidence and the submission-rejection-re-submission merry-go-round of work that becomes as exhausting as it is frustrating.

The system taught in this book can, if applied, totally eliminate these problems. In order to work to such a system a police officer must have:

1. A sound knowledge of the law.
2. A sound knowledge of statutory procedures (i.e. powers, requirements, restraints, etc.).
3. A mastery of the four operational police skills.
4. An understanding of the two main responsibilities he or she has in respect of all incidents.
5. A recognisable system which enables the officer to use (1), (2) and (3) above in order to fulfil (4) above.

This book is designed to teach (3) and (5).

The four operational police skills

Complete mastery of the four operational police skills is essential if you are to operate effectively. Such a mastery is of no less importance than that afforded to those who, in other occupations or professions, acquire diplomas or certificates as proof of their proficiency.

The four skills

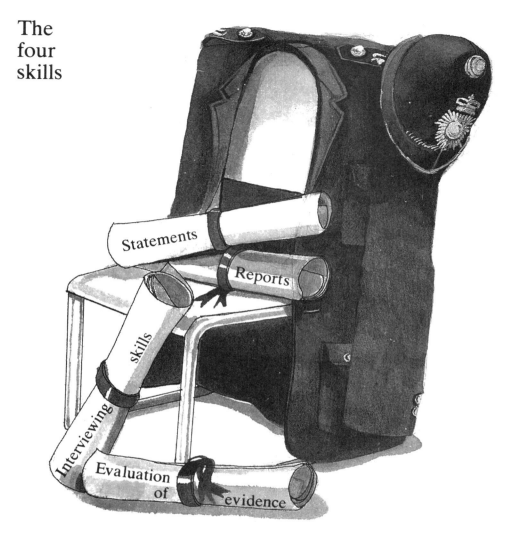

The four police skills I have been referring to above are:

1. **The making and taking of statements to the highest required level.**
2. **The compilation and construction of reports and files to the highest required level.**
3. **Skill in interviewing to an acceptable level.**
4. **Skill in the investigation and evaluation of incidents to an acceptable level.**

This book has been specifically written to teach these four skills and a system by which the skills can best be used. If you adopt and follow the teaching, you will find that you are in possession of a method of working which will guide you from the very first moments at the scene of any incident right through to the submission of a report/statement/file. The work you will then be capable of producing will be sufficient in content and design for presentation at all courts, up to and including Crown courts.

In addition you will discover you are in possession of a system which:

1. Produces high quality work with the minimum of supervision or checking.
2. Covers *any* incident you are likely to meet.
3. Will be applicable throughout the whole of your service.
4. Provides a firm base for higher training in operational police skills.

For the very first time in police training this book teaches you *how to do the job*.

How does it work?

First of all I should like to make it clear that this book is not just concerned with paperwork, far from it. You will find that much of the book is concerned with *how an officer should think at a particular stage in an enquiry*. The system teaches that the correct method of thought will naturally lead to a correct procedure being followed.

In the same way that a computer, once it has been correctly programmed, can cope with a myriad of problems, so you, armed with a mastery of the four operational police skills *plus* a dependable and flexible system of using them, will find that you can operate effectively and efficiently in all kinds of situations.

The four skills have been separated under the headings **'Statements'**, **'Reports'**, **'Interviewing skills'** and **'Evaluating evidence'**.

Having said that, I recognise that the beauty of operational police work is that it is virtually impossible to disconnect one procedure from another and say either that one is more important than the others or that one should be dealt with first before moving on to the next. The plain fact of the matter is that each procedure is important and is affected by and affects the other three.

This book takes this into account and introduces you, step-by-step, to the four skills. The teaching on each is complete in itself but, like operational police work, each skill is interdependent upon the others.

It should come as no surprise to you therefore to learn that only when you encounter the later chapters in the book will the overall picture begin to emerge. Towards the end of Chapter 7 on interviewing skills and throughout Chapter 8 concerned with the evaluation of evidence you will become much more aware of the wholeness of the system.

Part 1 covers the teaching of police skills. Part 2 contains examples of everything that is being taught. You will find that constant reference is made to Part 2 in the teaching text, and an indication on the pre-reading of these examples is given at the commencement of each chapter.

It is suggested that on first reading you follow the chapters in numerical order as the teaching is structured and unfolds with each successive chapter.

Upon completion, however, you will find that the book can then be dipped into at any point in order to refresh your memory or to use the many examples and specimens as aides from which to work.

Although officers these days have a greater access to transport, communications, specialised assistance, tape recorders, videos and a host of other aids, the actual doing of the job has changed little over the years. The two main responsibilities of the operational officer have remained constant for decades.

No matter what additional aids technology might have in store for you the system you are taught in this book can only enhance or be enhanced by it. That is the strength of the teaching.

2 Elementary statement construction

This chapter introduces you to the skill of **statement writing**, to a basic level, and covers the following areas:

1. The definition of a statement.
2. The three types of statement used in police work.
3. The definition and purpose of both an offence and an occurrence statement.
4. A simple 'method of approach' to *all* incidents.
5. Some statement writing rules.

This chapter deals with the first of the police skills, namely the writing of statements, albeit to a basic level. Although the chapter is complete in itself the procedures outlined in it are very much a basis for the three other skills. A mastery of the objectives in this chapter is important and will make the subsequent chapters that much easier to understand.

What is a statement?

A statement is a document, made by or taken from a person, containing details of the knowledge that person has of an incident.

Statements are merely written accounts of what people have experienced but they should never be undisciplined, rambling stories. Remember the best statements contain only *relevant* information and are constructed on a systematic approach to the collection of facts. It is that disciplined systematic approach to statement building with which this chapter is concerned.

There are only three types of statement used in police work. These are:

1. Offence statements (these include all crime and traffic offences).
2. Occurrence statements (e.g. civil dispute, sudden death and others).
3. Caution statements.

It may come as a surprise to be told that there are only three types of statement used in police work, but it is true. I would suggest that it is pointless to try to place statements into a variety of different categories based upon types of offences (e.g. indecent assault statements, burglary statements or careless driving statements). Each case you deal with is different and what might be sufficient for one indecent assault could well not even be applicable in another. This variety, of course, is part of the attraction of operational police work.

There are matters dealt with by the police which do not amount to offences and in those instances occurrence statements are completed. These will be dealt with later in the chapter. This book does not advise on the taking of Caution statements.

An offence statement

An offence statement is a written record of a person's first-hand knowledge of an incident which, as far as practicable, contains:

1. The factual detail, namely
    (a) the exact time, day, date and place of an alleged offence; and
    (b) the identification of the alleged offender.
2. The offence detail, namely
    sufficient evidence to prove the alleged offence, commonly known as 'points to prove'.

The factual detail

The first part of the definition is important primarily for the phrase '...first-hand knowledge...'. As far as the teaching on statement content in this chapter is concerned this means only those things which a person has experienced by use of the five senses. Thus in simple offence statements the following phrases would appear:

> 'At time, day, date and place I was on duty when *I saw* a motor car/ *I heard* the sound of an audible warning instrument/ *I smelt* smoke coming from the shop/ *I felt* a blow to my face/ *I tasted* a liquid....'

Moving on in the definition you encounter the first main requirement of *any* offence statement, i.e. the factual detail.

In the same way that lines of longitude and latitude 'fix' a person's position on the globe, so factual detail will 'fix' a person in time and at a location as the following example illustrates. First the '...time, day, date and place....'

'At 7.30 p.m. on Sunday, 1st April 19 — — I was on duty on The Strand, FOLKSTONE....'

The factual detail is completed by adding '...the identification of the alleged offender...' to the statement, thus:

'At 9.00 p.m. on Wednesday, 24th August 19 — — I was on duty in Leeds Road, HARROGATE when I saw *the defendant WILLIAMS*....'

A point to remember here is that a police officer may not discover the name of an offender until after he has stopped a vehicle or some minutes after an incident has taken place. Nevertheless it is quite acceptable to include a defendant's name in an offence statement, even though that name was not known by the officer until later in the incident. The previous example illustrates this technique.

There are other ways of identifying an alleged offender in an offence statement, as follows:

> 'The man who hit me *"was wearing a blue jumper, blue jeans and had a sandy coloured crew cut..."* or *"...was driving a yellow sports car..."* or *"...I later saw being taken away by the police..."* or *"...I know to be Jim CURTIS, I have known him for several years...".'*

These additional methods of identification *within a statement*, will be covered later in the book, but you should be aware they exist. At this stage, however, in simple offence statements, the phrase 'the defendant' followed by a surname will be sufficient.

Having 'fixed' an alleged offender in time and place in the offence statement it is then necessary to prove the commission of an offence. This is done, quite simply, by including in the statement the second specific type of detail.

The offence detail

Most offences, however involved, when examined are merely lists of points which need to be proved. For example, the simple offence of driving without a driving licence contains only five **points to prove**: namely, driving/a motor vehicle/on a road/without a driving licence/for that class of vehicle.

Thus in order to construct a simple offence statement proving that a particular person has committed that offence, the statement must contain the factual detail *plus* the offence detail (points to prove). The following illustration shows how simply this can be achieved.

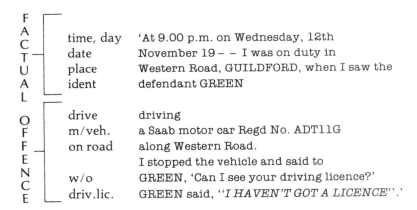

F A C T U A L	time, day date place ident	'At 9.00 p.m. on Wednesday, 12th November 19 – – I was on duty in Western Road, GUILDFORD, when I saw the defendant GREEN
O F F E N C E	drive m/veh. on road w/o driv.lic.	driving a Saab motor car Regd No. ADT11G along Western Road. I stopped the vehicle and said to GREEN, 'Can I see your driving licence?' GREEN said, "*I HAVEN'T GOT A LICENCE*".'

The **jigsaw** which shows how simply *all* offence statements are comprised of two types of detail, interlocking to form the whole, is an *aide-mémoire* I would commend to you.

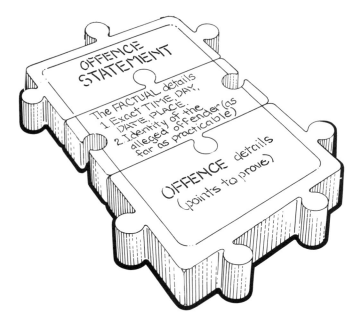

This simple illustration is the template for *all* offence statements you will ever encounter. Upon this uncomplicated design you will, in time, build the most involved of statements covering the more serious or complicated of offences. *Never forget*, however, that the basic design of factual detail plus offence detail remains constant and is vital to good offence statement construction. *Always apply it.*

Bearing in mind the jigsaw design look now at the next two examples and see how '...as far as practicable...' each offence statement conforms to the design.

STATEMENT FORM

Name .... Elizabeth WILLIAMS ....

Address .... 6 Cedar Grove, DAWLISH, Devon ....

Occupation... Housewife ....   Age .. 29 yrs. (b.16.5.54)

This statement (consisting of   1   pages each signed by me) is true to the best of my knowledge and belief and I make it knowing that if it is tendered in evidence I shall be liable to prosecution if I have wilfully stated in it anything which I know to be false or do not believe to be true.

Dated the.. 21st ....day of.. July .... 19--....   ....

Signed.... E. WILLIAMS ....

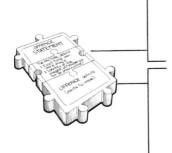

     At 3.25 p.m. on Thursday, 21st July 19--, I was driving my Ford Cortina motor car, Regd No. TDV 777R, along the main A30 EXETER to HONITON road, towards HONITON.

     I had just left the EXETER built-up area, when I was overtaken by an Austin Metro motor car, Regd No. AOD 266Y.

     I immediately saw that both direction indicators were flashing simultaneously, and continued to do so.

     After a few hundred yards I pulled into a lay-by at HONITON CLYST and rang the police.

     I could see the Metro was being driven by a man, but I cannot describe him. I do not think I would recognise him again.

Signed.. E. WILLIAMS ....

The relevance of the phrase '...as far as practical...' in the definition can now be seen. It sometimes happens, as in this case, that one person cannot provide *all* the necessary factual detail and offence detail. In this instance Elizabeth WILLIAMS is unable to identify the alleged offender but, *as far as practicable*, she provides as much detail as she is able.

Now read the following statement, from the police officer and see how he is able to add the missing evidence.

STATEMENT FORM

Name .... Brian John McCREERY

Address .... Devon and Cornwall Constabulary, EXETER, Devon

Occupation ..... Police..Constable..689 .... Age ...Over.21..years ......

This statement (consisting of 1 pages each signed by me) is true to the best of my knowledge and belief and I make it knowing that if it is tendered in evidence I shall be liable to prosecution if I have wilfully stated in it anything which I know to be false or do not believe to be true.

Dated the ...21st... day of ......July...................... 19...--...... ....

Signed .... B.J. McCREERY   P.C. 689 ....

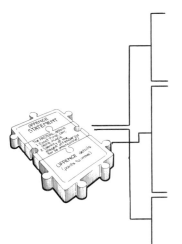

At 3.30 p.m. on Thursday, 21st July 19--, I was on motor patrol duty on the main A30 EXETER to HONITON road, when as a result of information received, I went to the ROCKBEARE straight.

I there saw an Austin Metro motor car, Regd No. AOD 266Y, being driven along the main road towards HONITON.

I saw that both the nearside and offside indicators were flashing simultaneously, as if being used as a hazard warning.

After following for approximately a quarter of a mile, I was able to stop the vehicle and found the driver to be the defendant Thomas WHITMORE.

I said to WHITMORE, 'As a result of a report from a member of the public, I have just followed your car, for approximately a quarter of a mile. I have seen that both the offside and nearside direction indicators have been flashing simultaneously, as if being used as a hazard warning. It is an offence for the indicators to be so used, unless the vehicle is stationary.'

WHITMORE said, 'I left them on, I'm sorry'.

I said, 'You will be reported for this offence'.

WHITMORE said, 'I didn't realise it was wrong, I'm sorry'.

Signed .... B. J. McCREEY   P.C. 689 ....

Before leaving this objective two important points are worth mentioning.

1. The factual detail will differ with every case.
2. The offence detail will always remain the same.

Let me explain, with the following example.

You, as an operational officer, deal with a number of people who fail to comply with the same stop sign, all during the same day. Although the *day*, *date* and *place* will be the same for each offender, the *time* and the *identity of the alleged offender* will be different.

However, in *all* cases the offence detail or points to prove remain exactly the same, i.e. driving/a motor vehicle/on a road/and failing to conform/with the indication given by a stop sign.

Having constructed an offence statement, how is it then used?

The purpose of an offence statement is:

1. **To provide sufficient information so that a decision can be made concerning the possible prosecution of an alleged offender.**
2. **If necessary to be used as a source of evidence in any subsequent proceedings.**

A decision whether to prosecute or not cannot be made unless the offence statements you submit contain sufficient evidence to support a prosecution. The *very least* a decision maker requires from you in such statements will be factual detail plus offence detail. If these two minimum requirements are not met then a decision cannot be made.

You should also be aware of the fact that if a decision to prosecute is made, your offence statements will be the source of evidence, relied upon in a court of law, to support that prosecution. In other words, your work will be subject to public scrutiny and it must, from the outset, be correct.

It is important, therefore, that your statements are always *accurate, relevant* and, above all, *truthful*. The truth, be it for or against the alleged offender, is always of prime importance in police work.

Now that you know what constitutes a basic offence statement, and its importance, it is equally necessary for you to understand how best to use that knowledge operationally.

To many students reading this book, operational work will be either an unknown or, at best, novel exprience. Officers young in service are often amazed at the ease with which their more experienced colleagues carry out their duties.

How is it that experienced officers, when confronted with obvious chaos and disorder, are able to produce evidence in the form of good statements, sufficient for a court of law?

The answer is quite simple, *they work to a system*. It is that system, used by the best of operational officers, which is the core of this book and which we will now begin to examine.

Method of approach

When an experienced officer arrives at the scene of any incident he *always thinks in a certain way* and it is that thought process that is the secret to working correctly.

If the correct thought process is followed it will naturally lead to the correct procedure being adopted when subsequently writing a statement about the incident. In this book that thought process is referred to as the **method of approach** and in truth if you follow it you will begin to *think like a police officer*.

The beauty of this system is that it starts you off in the correct way, *whatever the incident*. The method of approach works simply by asking yourself four short questions (see below):

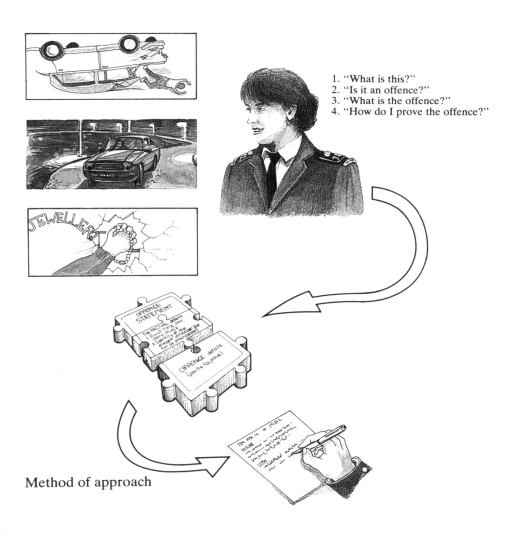

1. "What is this?"
2. "Is it an offence?"
3. "What is the offence?"
4. "How do I prove the offence?"

Method of approach

Although these four questions will now be examined in detail you will find, with experience, that you naturally answer them within seconds of arrival at the scene of a real incident.

In order to understand the method of approach consider how you would think upon attendance at the following two incidents:

— A fatal road accident on a busy road.
— A car being driven, at night, without lights.

'What is this?'

Upon arrival at any incident, offence or non-offence, you will attempt to categorise that incident, defining its seriousness. You will decide quickly whether assistance is required, does a threat of violence or danger to life exist or, as is often the case, is it a matter with which you alone can cope?

The answer to the first question in the method of approach is to categorise the incident in your mind.

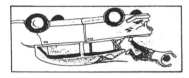

"What is this?"

Busy road — danger to me and others — serious accident — death — injuries need help — ambulance, breakdown — more officers.

Answer: 'This is serious, I need assistance.'

Minor incident — stop vehicle — check driver.

'This is apparently simple, I can manage alone.'

'Is it an offence?'

This second question is asked for two reasons. First, if you decide that there is a possibility of an offence, then a whole range of powers may become available (e.g. to demand documents, take into care, search, enter premises, arrest, etc.).

Secondly, if it is thought to be an offence incident it may well have a bearing on the manner in which the officer, you, approach those involved and their subsequent attitude to you.

Obviously if the incident does not constitute an offence most of the powers available to you will not apply.

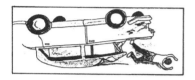
"Is it an offence?"

What happened here?
Is anyone at fault? Who?
Answer: 'Possibly'

It looks as if there
might be an offence/offences.
'Probably'

'What is the offence?'

Having decided that an incident is one involving the commission of an offence, you must then identify *exactly* what offence or offences have been committed. You are then in a position to decide positively on the precise powers available to you. In other words, as well as deciding on a particular offence, this question triggers in your mind the options open to you when dealing with the incident.

Further, and this is equally important, it is only after identifying the offence(s) that you can move on to the last question in the method of approach.

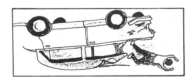
"What is the offence?"

Car driver reckless —
at fault — passenger
dead — possibly arrest —
breath test — inspect
vehicle.

Answer:'Causing death by
reckless driving.'

After lighting up
time, no lights —
simple process —
demand documents.

'Driving motor car without
lights.'

'How do I prove the offence?'

Whatever the offence this fourth question in the method of approach naturally leads you to the jigsaw, which in turn directs you to exactly what you need to do.

"How do I prove the offence?"

Answer: Factual detail:
At time, day, date and place,
the defendant...
Plus Offence detail: caused
the death/of [name]/by driving/
a motor vehicle/on a road/
recklessly.

Factual detail: At time,
day, date and place the
defendant...
Plus Offence detail:
driving/a motor vehicle/
on a road/during the hours
of darkness/without obligatory
lights.

Despite the mayhem and distress at the fatal accident, by using the method of approach you will act as calmly and efficiently as when dealing with the relatively simple incident of a car without lights.

Remember   *This system is common to all offences and will always work for you.*

By applying this system, at the scene of an incident, you, as an operational officer, are now meeting your two main responsibilities in restoring the peace and beginning to convert that incident into such a form (statements) that a decision can be made as to the participants in that incident.

There are, of course, matters requiring action by the police, which do not amount to offences. Although in most instances only a report is prepared, there are occasions when statements are taken. These are known as ocurrence statements.

What are occurrence statements?

An occurrence statement is a written record of an incident, which contains all the relevant knowledge the person making the statement has of it. It can include hearsay and evidence of opinion.

The purpose of an occurrence statement is to convey to the reader all the relevant knowledge the person making the statement has of the incident.

Sudden deaths are the incidents which most frequently require occurrence statements, but so do such happenings as illness or accidents in the street and civil or domestic disputes.

Again at the scene of such incidents you will use the method of approach, but in answer to Question (2), 'Is it an offence?', your answer will be, 'No'. The last two questions in the method of approach, therefore, do not apply. However, you will then ask the question, 'Should someone need, or want, to know about this?'

Such a person could be a coroner (sudden death, illness in the street), a recorder in a civil court (dispute over property or land), an official in a local government department (complaint about road defect, noise) or a judge in a divorce court (domestic dispute).

Read the example of an occurrence statement on page 22 and note the following points:

1. There is no set format, as was found in the offence statement, the person making the statement simply tells what has happened.
2. Both hearsay and opinion have been included and so they should be, *if they are thought to be relevant,* or possibly of some assistance to the person reading.
3. Consider what agencies might be interested in such a statement (immediate supervisors, possibly a coroner, insurance company or a civil court).
4. Note how this comparatively serious incident has been positively classified as non-offence, by one short occurrence statement, although, as you will see later, other similar statements might well be taken.

STATEMENT FORM

Name .... Phillip James HARDCASTLE

Address .... 50 Otley Road, LEEDS, Yorkshire

Occupation. Managing Director .... Age .... 50 yrs (b.20.5.33)

This statement (consisting of 2 pages each signed by me) is true to the best of my knowledge and
belief and I make it knowing that if it is tendered in evidence I shall be liable to prosecution if I have
wilfully stated in it anything which I know to be false or do not believe to be true.

Dated the .... 1st .... day of .... July .... 19 .-- . ...

Signed...... P.J. HARDCASTLE

At 12.30 p.m. on Friday, 1st July 19--,
I was walking with my wife Angela in Fore Street, ST IVES,
Cornwall, where we were spending a few days on holiday.
At that time we were outside the Castle public house.

I was looking at the menu, on the wall, by the
pub doorway, when my wife said, 'Oh my God Phil, I think
that man is going to fall'.

Right away I looked around and saw a man on
some scaffolding, outside CURNOWS' gift shop. He was
quite high up, I would think about 20 to 25 feet from
the ground, and he was carrying a large number of
roofing tiles.

He looked as though he had lost his balance,
because he was swaying around, like a tight-rope walker,
with the tiles slipping from his hands.

Then he fell off the scaffolding, on to the
roadway. It looked as though he landed on his left
shoulder.

My wife and I went across to the man and I
saw he was bleeding from the left side of his head. He
was unconscious and quite pale.

My wife ran off to phone for the ambulance and
while I was waiting for it to arrive a large man in
overalls and flat cap came over. I think he was the
foreman. He had a thin black moustache and he was wearing
a donkey jacket with a name, which I can't remember,
stencilled on the back of the jacket.

Signed......... P.J. HARDCASTLE ....

22

I heard him say to somebody, something about the man I had seen fall had been told before about carrying too many tiles.

There was no one else on the scaffolding or near the man when he fell, and in my opinion it was an accident.

The man who fell was in his mid-20s, slim build, with gingerish hair and he was wearing the same kind of donkey jacket as the big man I have already described.

My wife didn't actually see the man fall because she had her hands over her eyes at the time.

Signed .... P.J.HARDCASTLE ....

Statement writing rules

The following are a number of rules which, it is suggested, should be complied with in relation to both offence and occurrence statements.

1. *All statements must be written in ink.* Compliance with this rule negates any later claim that a statement has been altered.
2. *Locations and surnames to be in BLOCK capitals.* This is a common-sense suggestion and is already accepted police practice in most police offices.
3. *No police jargon. As far as practicable the person's own words to be used.* Always avoid the trap of using police jargon which is the slightly pompous 'I was proceeding' type of language. If a person uses slang or colloquial expressions, include it in the statement with, if it is required, an explanation.
4. *All errors crossed through with a single line and initialled by the person making the statement. No erasures.*
5. *Each page must be signed by the person making the statement.*
6. *Where relevant 'direct speech' to be included. All replies from the offender to be in BLOCK CAPITALS.* Ensure that where important dialogue has taken place and is recorded in a statement, as far as possible, such dialogue is recorded in 'direct speech' as the following examples illustrate:
    RIGHT   I said, 'Can I see your driving licence?'
            The defendant JAMES said, 'I'M SORRY OFFICER, I HAVEN'T GOT ONE'.*
    WRONG   I asked the defendant JAMES for his driving licence and he told me he didn't have one.
7. *If the person making the statement cannot read then the statement will be read over to that person and this fact noted on the statement by the officer taking it.*
8. *Person making the statement must sign the declaration on the statement, regarding its truthfulness.*
9. *The officer taking the statement will sign it with his name, rank and number.*
10. *The normal rules of English grammar will apply.*

Conclusion

In addition to identifying the different types of statement used in police work, and their purpose, this chapter has introduced you to two important procedures, namely: the manner of construction of *all* offence statements; and the method of approach to *all* incidents.

These two procedures, in particular, are of prime importance to you as they form the basis for your further learning in operational police skills.

---

* For ease of reading, replies by offenders have been underlined in this book and are not in block capitals.

Improving your skills

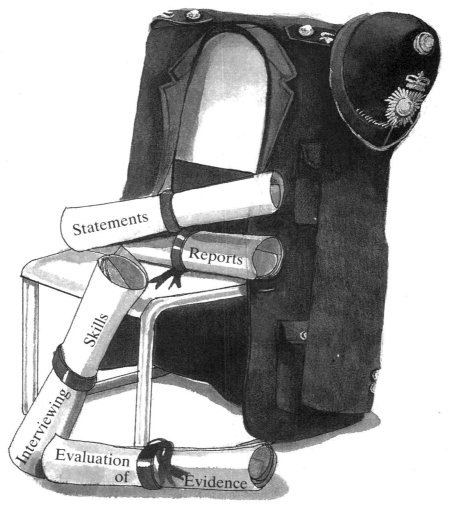

Look again at the two examples of offence statements, on pages 13 and 15, and note the following points:

1. Observe the simple layout of most basic offence statements (i.e. those concerned with simple offences). They are almost always built along these simple lines.
2. There is a marked lack of irrelevant or unnecessary detail. You should not now be suprised to discover how little is required to prove an offence, provided the method of approach is followed. Good statements are slim but sufficient.
3. There is no hearsay included. Although later in the book you will be told of instances where hearsay can be included, as a general rule, do not include hearsay in basic offence statements. Certainly you will find, in practice, that such simple statements seldom, if ever, require the inclusion of such evidence.
4. In the offence statement of WILLIAMS note how, although she cannot positively identify the offender, as far as practicable, she tries to do so, stating that the driver, she thinks, was a man.

3 Complex statement construction

You will find, from this point onwards, that continual reference is made to the three specimen reports, A, B and C, in Part 2 of the book. It is suggested that in order to obtain the maximum benefit from the teaching text you familiarise yourself with the statements within those reports, before continuing.

This chapter continues the teaching of the skill of statement writing, but to a higher level, and is concerned very much with building upon the simple system of offence statement construction you were introduced to in Chapter 2. The following areas are covered:

1. The inclusion, in offence statements, of hearsay, opinion and relevant facts in addition to points to prove.
2. Linking exhibits with statements.
3. The importance of supporting evidence.
4. Defences.
5. The importance of negative statements.

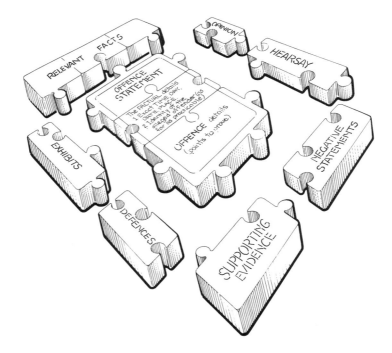

In Chapter 2 you were shown the simplest of offence statements, dealing with uncomplicated, simple offences, which conformed to the basic jigsaw design and no more. However, continually you will be confronted with incidents requiring more complex statements, containing an increased amount of detail. This chapter introduces those important 'add-ons', but remember the basic template of factual detail plus offence detail must be adhered to for without it there is no firm base upon which to build these more complex statements.

Although it may appear that the statements you will now be examining are less disciplined in their design and content, nothing could be further from the truth. You will discover no *irrelevancies, duplications* or *aimless comment* in these statements, rather you will find, after completing this chapter, that you will be able not only to recognise *what* has been included and classify it, but also *why* it has been so included.

Opinion

Usually **opinion** is not included in offence statements, however, there are five instances in law where it can be so included:

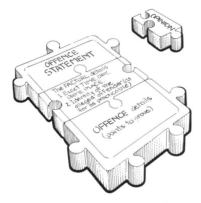

1. Statements from recognised experts in science, art and trade

Experts in science, art and trade are allowed to give evidence of opinion but only on subjects about which they are expert. Further, before giving such an opinion it must be 'proved' within the offence statement that they are such experts. This is done simply by including a paragraph or two, usually at the beginning of the statement, outlining the expert's qualifications and experience. This extract from the statement of Peter DENSHAM (Report C, page 171) illustrates this procedure.

'I am a doctor of medicine, having studied at the LEEDS University and qualified in 1981. Since that time I have been resident at the LEEDS Royal Infirmary and am currently the senior casualty officer, at that hospital.'

The next four uses of opinion in offence statements are much more common.

2. Opinion as to a person's...

Identity

'*...I think the man I saw* breaking into my house *was Fred WILLIAMS*, who lives in our street....'

Condition

'...the girl looked frightened, dreadfully white and distressed, as if she was in shock. *In my opinion she was obviously upset....*'

Age

'...I would describe the youth who stole my watch *as about 19 to 20 years, no older, in my opinion....*'

In the specimen reports at the rear of the book you will find many examples of these three uses of opinion.

---

3. Opinion as to a thing's...

Identity

'...the wallet I saw the man holding *looked like my father's wallet....*'

Condition

'*The car in my opinion was in a very poor condition*, rusty, dirty and generally in a delapidated state.'

Age

'It's difficult to say exactly, but the *knife looked quite old*, as if it had been used before. *It didn't look new to me.*'

---

4. Opinion as to the appearance of illness or drunkenness

Within months of taking up operational duties, evidence of opinion as to drunkenness and, to a lesser extent, illness, will have become commonplace in your offence statements. This extract from the statement of William GRIGG (Report C, page 170) illustrates the use of opinion as to drunkenness. He is not a police officer or an expert but his evidence is important and pertinent.

'I got the impression that he was slightly drunk. He was shouting loudly, smelling strongly of drink and his speech was slightly slurred. However, he wasn't that drunk, because he quietened down very quickly when the police arrived.'

Illness

'When I got to the car I could see the driver slumped over the wheel, his face was a bluish colour. *He looked very sick to me.*'

5. Opinion as to the speed of motor vehicles

The evidence of the opinion of two police officers as to the speed of a vehicle is still accepted as proof of excess speed. However, the use of such evidence is very rare these days. What is more common is evidence of opinion by members of the public of the speed of vehicles, as in this extract from the statement of William BOUNDY (Report B, page 142).

'At this time I was doing about 35 m.p.h. and I would estimate the speed of the MGB to be only a little above that, perhaps 40 to 45 m.p.h. He was certainly taking a long time to overtake me.'

In the same report the statements of RELPH and UPTON (pages 136-140) both contain similar examples of this type of evidence of opinion.

Practical note   Opinion as to *why something happened.*

Although not always allowable in a court, it has become generally accepted practice to include such opinion in offence statements. The two extracts from the statements of OAKDEN and GRIGG (Report C, pages 166 and 169) illustrate how such evidence is included.

'I cannot say why this assault took place, there seemed to be no reason for it at all.'

'I have no idea why this fight took place, except to suppose it was about someone queue jumping.'

Hearsay evidence

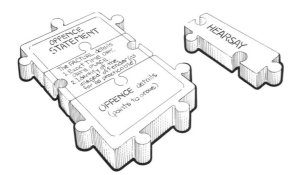

In Chapter 2 I stated that as a general rule you do not include **hearsay** in offence statements but added that you would be told of instances when hearsay could be so included. Let me explain.

It is important that you know exactly what constitutes hearsay evidence and are aware, almost by second nature, that it is such evidence. It should jar against your sensibilities when you meet it. Only by knowing precisely what hearsay is are you able to exclude it. Similarly, by knowing it so well, you will now know *when* it is being included in offence statements.

There are occasions when hearsay can be included in offence statements, some examples of which are as follows:

1. Oral statements by the Accused.
2. Oral statements made in the presence and hearing of the Accused.
3. Early complaint in sexual offences.

The admissibility of hearsay under points (1) and (2) above is only logical and you will find many examples of this in the specimen reports.

In relation to (3), Early complaint in sexual offences, the law allows that certain things said by a victim of a sexual assault to a person other than the Accused can be admissible. Such evidence tends to show that there was no consent to the alleged act, not that the Accused was guilty.

A person to whom a girl has fled, following a sexual attack, would include the following passage in an offence statement, to record the early complaint.

'...when I opened the door I saw a young woman standing there. She was crying and distressed and said to me, *"Please help me, I've been raped".'*

Note that when including the early complaint, the 'direct speech' is recorded as the above example illustrates.

Hearsay in practice

It is now common practice in most forces for all *relevant* hearsay to be included in offence statements that officers take. If such hearsay is thought, at a later date, to be inadmissible, it can be edited by legal advisers.

It must be stressed that this is not a free-for-all approach to the inclusion of hearsay being advocated. The rule of thumb which will guide you is:

— If the hearsay is *relevant, but only if it is relevant,* then include it.
— Hearsay evidence is *never included* in statements *made by police officers,* unless under (1), (2) or (3) above.

There are many examples of the inclusion of *relevant* hearsay in the offence statements in the specimen reports A to C. However, I would draw your attention to these two extracts from the statement of UPTON. The first is irrelevant and should not have been included while the second extract, although it may not be ultimately admissible in court, is a correct inclusion of relevant hearsay in an offence statement (page 139).

'I remember Dr RELPH said, "It's been a busy day but a most successful day, so far".'

'Dr RELPH said, "*Bloody idiot, he's going to hit us*", or "*He's not going to make it*", or words to that effect.'

The second part of the rule of thumb, listed above, makes it clear that hearsay is never included in statements *made* by police officers. The kind of inclusion *not* required from you is to be found in this extract from the statement of ALFORD (Report C, page 175).

'Constable TURNER said, "Looks like a big crowd in the Crypt tonight. We'd better see the place out".'

The inclusion of hearsay in the offence statements you *take*, therefore, requires the same disciplined thinking you have been applying to the more simple statements discussed in Chapter 2.

RELEVANT FACTS in addition to POINTS TO PROVE

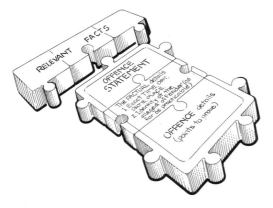

This objective lists a number of points that will be obvious to you as being most relevant to any possible prosecution. Common sense should dictate to you that these additional relevant facts are important, not only for the information of a decision maker, but very much for the information of a court. Further, they will often flesh out the basic skeleton of factual detail plus offence detail and can greatly strengthen a case.

Remember, however, *you* are the person with the knowledge of a particular case and *you* are the one who decides what is relevant and whether it is then included in an offence statement.

Introductory and explanatory facts

These **relevant facts** are usually required when introducing an expert in an offence statement. This procedure has already been explained earlier. It can also mean, however, the inclusion of relevant facts introducing a person who is not one of the recognised experts. The first paragraph of the offence statement of BOUNDY (Report B, page 141) is an example of this kind of evidence, as this man's driving experience is most certainly relevant to this particular case, which involves a road accident. Had he been making a statement about a theft case, such a paragraph would not have appeared.

'I am employed as a driver by WALDRON, CHANNON and HOPKINS, road hauliers of CHELTENHAM and have been driving heavy lorries, both in this country and on the Continent, for the past twenty-five years.'

Examples of the wrong use of the 'introductory paragraph' can be found liberally sprinkled among the specimen reports, but I would particularly draw your attention to the two following extracts. This utterance by HINDLE (Report B, page 144) is obviously totally irrelevant to this particular case.

'I am an unemployed hotel worker, having been previously employed in large hotels, as a kitchen porter, in the North of England. Since June 1965 I have been unemployed.'

Similarly, Constable ADAMS has listed in this paragraph (Report B, page 146) all the details to be found on the heading of the statement. Why repeat them in this irrelevant, time-consuming duplication?

'I am a Police Constable of the Avon and Somerset Constabulary, currently stationed at Downend, BRISTOL.'

Opportunity

This is a most important relevant fact in that it often needs to be shown in a prosecution that a person had the physical ability to carry out the unlawful act alleged. Examples of **opportunity** are the physical proximity of a person to another (assault), access to property (theft) or the only person in the house with a child (child abuse). In the assault case (Report C) you will find examples of the physical proximity of the offender to the victim as in this extract from the statement of OAKDEN (page 164) which leaves no doubt as to the Accused's ability to carry out an assault.

'when I heard the man in front, say something like, "*You've been bloody queue jumping mate*", or words to that effect. He appeared to be talking to the person immediately in front of him, another young man, who was wearing a sports jacket.'

Motive

Often the **motive** for the commission of an offence is provided by the Accused, when interviewed, and such evidence is telling, invariably accounting for a person's behaviour. This type of relevant fact is not always considered but it does exist and would appear in an offence statement in the following form:
(Landlord who has discovered a gas meter broken into, complaining about the occupant of the flat)

'...and when I checked the meter I found the lock had been broken and money missing. I do know that Tony TIMMS has been short of money, only two days ago he asked if he could borrow £5 to buy some food....'

Preparation to commit crime

The relevant evidence of a **preparation to commit crime** usually prompts mental images of a gang arming themselves with masks and sawn-off shotguns and secreting getaway cars in quiet lock-ups. Although indeed these are classic examples of preparatory acts you will come across much more commonplace instances in your day-to-day duty, as the following shows:
(Police officer's statement outlining action after arresting a football hooligan)

'...I then took HENTHORNE to a nearby police van and before placing him in the van I searched him and found, in the back pocket of his jeans, a sketch plan of the football stadium, showing locations of the visiting supporters and parking points for the visiting coaches...'

There is no similar relevant evidence to be found in the specimen reports except perhaps these two extracts from the statements of OAKDEN (page 165)

'and then I saw him take a bottle from his jacket pocket. It was an empty Newcastle Brown Ale bottle.'

and GRIGG (page 168) from the assault report.

'Suddenly I saw the man in the leather jacket take an empty beer bottle from a jacket pocket.'

The fact that such a weapon (an empty beer bottle) was in the man's pocket is such unusual conduct that it has been properly included and could be said to show a preparation to commit crime.

Conduct of accused/victim

Offenders often act in a way or say things that are in accord with the commission of an offence and evidence of this **conduct** or speech is important. Simple everyday examples of such evidence are the hurried flight from the scene of a crime or the furtive hiding of property. There are many examples of this relevant evidence in the specimen reports. These extracts from the statement of PATTINSON (Report C, page 161) show the impact of such evidence.

'I could smell intoxicating liquor on the man's breath and his speech was slightly slurred, but I didn't get the impression that he was drunk.'
 'The man just seemed belligerent and I got the impression he wanted to pick a fight with me.'
 'I then heard the man say, "Don't turn your back on me mate".'

Utterances made by an Accused at the scene of an incident are of great value, often proving intent, sometimes as admissions of guilt. They should, as far as practicable, be recorded in 'direct speech'. In the careless driving report (Report B) the statement of RELPH records the following admission from the alleged offender, 'I didn't see you until it was too late' (page 138), while in the assault report (Report C) PATTINSON records the alleged as saying, 'You bastard, I'm going to do you... I'll kill you, you bastard' (page 161). Consider the impact such evidence would have in a court.

The **conduct of the victim** is similarly important. People who have been wronged invariably react in a certain way. Where property has been stolen the loser will usually make a complaint as soon as the theft is discovered. Victims of sexual assaults can appear distressed, ashamed or embarrassed and the fact that they are should be included in the statements of the people who have seen them so.

The condition, attitude and conduct of the victim tend to support, or otherwise, any complaint, both in your mind and in the eyes of the court before which the case is to be heard.

This passage from the statement of GRIGG (page 168) gives an account of the victim's conduct prior to the assault

'I say this because he was raising his voice and swearing and shouting, while the other man was talking quietly and I didn't hear him swearing.'

Both GRIGG and OAKDEN in their statements (pages 164-170) describe the victim's conduct throughout the incident showing how he (the victim) does all he can to avoid violence. This evidence is most relevant.

Why something happened

This relevant fact, **why something happened**, is very similar to what you have already been taught concerning the inclusion of a person's *opinion* why something happened. In this instance, however, the person puts forward *facts* explaining why something happened. Again, this evidence is not always admissible in a court but if it exists should be included. These two extracts from the statements of UPTON (page 140) and BOUNDY (page 143) both contain reasons why something happened.

'This accident happened because the driver of the red car tried to overtake the lorry when there was not enough distance between the lorry and Dr RELPH'S car for him to do so.'

'This accident happened because the driver of the MGB totally misjudged his overtaking of my lorry.'

Those then are the five relevant facts in addition to points to prove you should always consider for inclusion in your offence statements.

Linking exhibits with statements

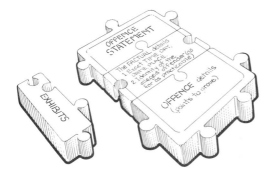

There are occasions when evidence is accepted by a court merely by the presentation of a statement to that court. This means that the person making the statement does not attend the court. If that person produces or refers to an exhibit how then is that exhibit to be produced to the court? The procedure is quite simple and is as follows:

The exhibit is given an identifying mark, which is usually the initials of the first person referring to it, followed by a number. Therefore, an exhibit produced by Angela Bridget COOGAN would be given the identifying mark ABC/1 and in her statement reference to the exhibit would appear thus:

'...the Accused pointed to a knife (ABC/1) and said, "THAT'S THE ONE...".'

A label is attached to the exhibit in this case the knife, bearing the same identifying mark (ABC/1) and the signature of COOGAN. Accordingly, both the label and statement bear the same identifying mark and signature.

Should COOGAN go on to refer to other exhibits in that statement the same initials are used but the number is changed, thus:

'...I later went into another part of the house with the Accused and in the lounge I saw a cassette recorder (ABC/2)....'

In the statements contained in the specimen reports in Part 2 you will find a host of examples of this most simple procedure.

It is most important to note that this procedure is *never used* in the body of a **caution statement** although, of course, once such a statement has been completed it becomes a documentary exhibit and is allocated an identifying mark as described above. The statement of Constable ADAMS (page 147) shows how a caution statement is allocated such a mark.

'Towards the end of the interview MORRIS elected to make a written statement under caution (GGA/3) which I wrote at his dictation.'

It is suggested you adopt this procedure concerning exhibits for *all* offence or occurrence statements you make or take, regardless of whether or not you anticipate the person's non-attendance at court. By doing so you will become adept at using this simple procedure.

Supporting evidence

This objective is designed to teach you how to preserve the strength of **supporting evidence** for, as you will quickly discover for yourself, *evidence of two is indeed stronger than evidence of one.*

In relation to all incidents the evidence of two or more persons, *independently taken,* is much stronger than the evidence of one.

In order to preserve that strength, the following procedures should be followed:

1. *The statements should, as far as practicable, be taken from each person, independently of one another.*
   If there are a number of witnesses to an incident ensure that each is interviewed separately and any subsequent statements taken independently of the others. In addition, try to prevent such persons conferring among themselves. Remember, evidence from one person which is supportive of another, *taken independently,* is invariably unshakeable.

2. *There should be no prompting, although correct, fair questioning, can be employed.*
   The manner in which you question suspects and non-suspects will be discussed in depth later, but you must ensure that you do not suggest answers when you pose questions. After all by questioning each person correctly you will know for sure that you are obtaining the truth and that must always be your goal.
   On occasions you will form a preconceived idea of what has happened which might not be correct. There will be a strong temptation for you to put questions in such a manner that the questions will conform to and support that preconceived idea. Never do this. Always, regardless of the consequences, *search for the truth.*

3. *The statement from each person should be full in content.*
This sub-heading means that the statements from each of the witnesses will be full complete accounts. You will not show the statement of A to B and then suggest to B that all he need say in a statement is, 'I have read the statement of A and corroborate what he says'. This is totally unacceptable.

Bear in mind that the Accused is not present when you are collecting this evidence and therefore he or she, whatever he or she has allegedly done, deserves to be properly represented. This is your responsibility and you discharge it by collecting the evidence in the correct manner.

The statements in the specimen reports contain many examples of supporting evidence and I would draw your attention particularly to the statements of OAKDEN and GRIGG (Report C, pages 164-170) dealing with the assault and those of RELPH and UPTON (Report B, pages 136-140) which refer to the road accident. See how, although taken independently, each statement tends, in each case, to support the other.

Defences

You will find, in relation to most offences, that almost invariably excuses, reasons or recognised **defences** exist. Some motoring offences, for example, allow for the fact that if the defect in a motor vehicle occurred on that particular journey, then it is a legitimate excuse. Similarly, sudden mechanical failure or unexpected illness (automatism) can negate a charge of careless or reckless driving. Some assaults are justifiable or lawful (due to provocation or self-defence) and in theft cases a person's appropriation of property need not necessarily be dishonest if that person genuinely believes he has a claim of right to the property.

'Is there a defence/excuse

for this offence.'

It is impossible to teach you the separate defences that exist for each offence, therefore, the system you are being taught allows for this in the following way. Refer back to Chapter 2 and consider again the four questions asked in the section 'Method of approach'. In order to cover any possible defence merely add one further question, namely, *'Is there a defence or excuse for this offence?'*

This extract from the statement of GRIGG (page 170) concerning the assault, illustrates how defences can be taken into account.

'Having said all that, the attack seemed totally unprovoked and there was no reason that I could see why the man in the leather jacket fought with the other man. There was certainly no reason to use the bottle.'

Negative statements

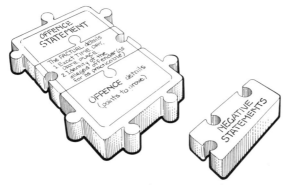

A negative statement is taken to record a person's denial of knowledge of an incident. It is used to rebut a later change of story by the person making the statement.

Although there are only three types of statement used in police work, there is a sub-heading of both offence and occurrence statements, namely negative statements.

In the course of the many investigations that lie in front of you there will be occasions when you will meet individuals not suspects, who will be most reluctant to give you any information. This may be because they are friends of the suspect or that they do not wish to be involved or that they do not particularly like the police. You are obliged, however, to search for the truth and it is suprising, simply by asking questions, how much information you can obtain from such people.

This extract from the statement of HINDLE (Report B, page 144) shows how the officer obtains useful information from a most reluctant witness.

'I have been asked if I saw anything of this accident and I can say I did not, I was asleep.

I have been asked if I can give any details of the speed of the lorry and I cannot.

I have been asked if I can give any details about a red MGB sports car and its overtaking of the lorry and I cannot.'

Note also how by the continued use of the phrase 'I have been asked...' the officer has plugged away at each individual point, eliciting some response from the person.

You will find this 'one point at a time' questioning technique referred to again in a later chapter, but you should be able to see already how effective it can be in obtaining a negative statement.

Of course, a person is not obliged to make a written statement and in such an instance it is suggested you ask the same questions, in the same manner, and record the questions and answers in your pocket notebook. At the end of the interview the person refusing to make a statement should be invited to sign the pocket notebook entry. The example on pages 111 − 112 illustrates this. Should this person later change his or her story such a pocket notebook entry can be produced to negate his or her story. The strength of such entries is that they are made *at the time or as soon as practicable after the event.*

Remember *Just because a person says he neither saw nor heard anything, does not mean that his or her story is worthless. Negative statements can be of great use.*

Conclusion

You have now completed all the instruction concerning **statement writing** , the first of the police skills.

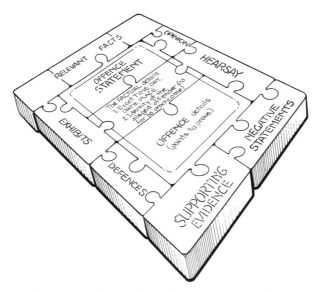

Be prepared for the fact that, to begin with, most incidents will appear complicated and insoluble but believe me they seldom are. By always applying the system you have been taught you will find your thinking becomes properly channelled. You will almost automatically start to apply the method of approach and all the subsequent add-ons you have been introduced to in this chapter.

If you do this you will become proficient in producing statements to the highest level and will have mastered one of the four operational police skills.

Improving your skills

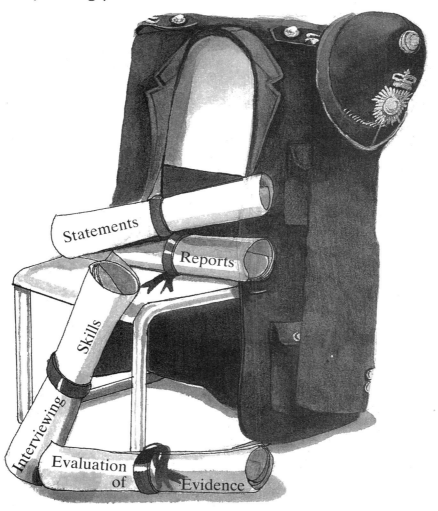

1. *Statement of COOPER* (page 117) **1
   Time and again in this and the other reports, the phrase 'in the presence and hearing of the Accused' crops up. It is most important that some things which are said are admissible and to facilitate this it must be proved that the Accused heard what was said. This is how to prove it.

2. *Statement of WILLS* (page 119) **2
   The phrase 'I would recognise (the defendant) again' crops up in all the reports. A decision maker needs to be aware of the strengths and weaknesses of witnesses, particularly in relation to the relevant fact of identification of the offender. *Do not forget to ask the witness if he or she would recognise the defendant.*

3. *Statement of LEWIS* (page 121) **3
    Often witnesses themselves will put forward reasons why they suddenly took an interest in a person or event. Include this in any statement they make, however irrational you may consider it to be. It is after all the truth and can be most telling in court.

4. *Statement of GRIGG* (page 170) **4
    The final sentence of this paragraph, which concerns opinion, is a direct quote from the witness and it speaks volumes.

5. *Statement of PATTINSON* (page 162) **5
    The phrase '...like a man with a sword would lunge...' is again a description proffered by the witness. It is graphic, spontaneous and should be included.

6. *Statement of RELPH* (page 137) **6
    The phrase '...the kind you see when a vehicle is under heavy braking...' is again an example of the actual words a witness has chosen to use to describe what has happened. Invariably you cannot improve on their descriptions, so don't try.

7. *Statement of RELPH* (page 137) **7
    Statement of UPTON (page 140) **8
    The last sentence of both these paragraphs, neatly *proves that the defendant was the driver.*

8. *Statement of RELPH* (page 136)
    This whole statement illustrates how an event, which probably lasted 15 to 20 seconds, can be described in the greatest of detail. A good tip is to 'stop the action' after a certain time (however small) and describe the scene, in this instance mentioning such things as positions of vehicles, speeds, etc., then move on a few seconds. This method is particularly helpful in describing the build-up to accidents or careless driving incidents.

9. *Statement of PATTINSON* (page 160)
    Another example of where the complainant is describing an incident which took probably less than 20 seconds to unfold, but the interviewing officer is again using the 'stop the action' technique and each blow and movement of the participants is being recorded.

10. *Statement of DENSHAM* (page 171) **9
    It is often necessary to show a weapon or an article to an expert witness, such as a doctor or a pathologist and, as in this case, their evidence can be most supportive. However, advice from supervisors must be sought before adopting such a course of action as precautions must be taken to avoid forensic 'contamination' of exhibits.

4 Report construction

This chapter is the first of three concerned with the skill of **report writing** and it covers the following points:

1. The definition, purpose and types of report used in police work.
2. 'Simple reports', their purpose and composition.
3. A preview of the more complex reports, known as 'full reports'.
4. A simple method of 'thinking it through' when organising one's thoughts before commencing any report.
5. Some report writing rules.

Reports, like statements, are very much tools of your trade and you should know how to *use* them correctly, easily and to good effect.

Crime or accident reports are representations of what has happened to members of the public who have become either a victim or an aggrieved. If your reports are deficient, poorly constructed or just downright bad then you have failed not only in your second responsibility, which is properly to present that incident in an acceptable form to a decision maker, but also you have failed the public. You are their only real link with the decision maker, their representative in the system of law and order in this country. Do not fail them.

Report writing is not a daunting task, it is merely a question of knowing *what* you are trying to achieve and *how* best to do it. As in Chapter 2, where you were introduced to the method of approach when constructing offence statements, so in this chapter you will discover a similar system of thinking it through when considering report construction.

There are only eight types of report used in police work and they vary in size and complexity. Most of them are simple in design and content. All of them are easy to construct.

What is a report?

A report is a written document of varying length and complexity which conveys information to a decision maker.

Within the police service the word report can mean a single sheet or a sheaf of papers and in this latter instance the terms **report** and **file** are synonymous. Therefore, in the above definition the word document includes the plural.

The phrase '...conveys information to a decision maker...' is important in that the type of information to be conveyed directly affects the type of report to be constructed. This will be illustrated later in the chapter.

It should be stated here that the final decision to prosecute any offence rests with the Crown Prosecution Service. However, most branches of that department have given tacit permission for the prosecution of the less serious offences to be approved within the police organisation. This book reflects that decision.

Having covered, in some detail in the previous chapters, the purpose and content of statements you could well ask what purpose reports serve?

The purpose of a report is to convey *information*:

(a)   where there are no statements; *or*
(b)   not allowed in statements; *and/or*
(c)   not included in statements; *and/or*
(d)   drawn from statements so as to assist in their being understood.

The phrase *'information*: (a) where there are no statements' is self-explanatory. Often, as you will see, there are instances where no statements will have been made or taken and a report, probably quite small, will suffice.

Points (b) to (d) will be fully considered later in Chapter 5, but you should remember this definition as, from it, you should be able to see that *reports are never duplications of statements*.

Reports can be divided into two main types: **simple reports** and **full reports** (often referred to, within the police service, as 'full files').

This chapter is mainly concerned with simple reports. You will be introduced to the various types of full reports, but Chapters 5 and 6 deal in depth with that subject.

Simple reports

There are four simple reports used in police work as follows:

Administrative report

This is a simple report from an officer to a department or individual within the police service, containing administrative information.

ASHTON .... Station

'D' .... Division

Eastern .... Area   30th April .... 19--......

Subject ....

Up-dating of personal record - birth of son

Officer Reporting .... Constable No. 77   J. EMMETT

To ..... Ch/Supt R. BAILEY ....   'D' .... Division

Sir,

On Monday, 28th April 19-- my wife gave birth to a son, Timothy Patrick EMMETT.

I ask that these details be added to my personal record.

Police Constable No. 77

Such reports are, as the example shows, simple in the extreme and are used merely for passing information either for record purposes or a certain course of administrative action. It is invariably directed towards a civilian administrator, who acts upon it or any recommendation thereon. Other examples of the use of this type of report are applications for a certain department/course/promotion board/appointment/station as well as the conveying of simple information. Truly a simple report.

Pro-forma report

This is a self-explanatory form, completed when recording details of certain types of incident, regularly brought to the attention of the police.

The commission of a crime or a road traffic accident are two of the more common incidents which are regularly reported to the police and, because of this, most forces have pre-printed forms, booklets or **pro-forma report** forms. All are completed mainly by answering questions posed on the form, ticking boxes or crossing through information not applicable. Each of the 43 forces in England and Wales has its own individual set of forms and they are used primarily for statistical or record purposes. Such pro-forma reports require only familiarity in becoming adept at their completion.

Duty report

This is a report, requested from an officer, detailing his actions during a specified period of duty.

CHELTENHAM .... Station

'B' .... Division

Northern .... Area   .... 12th April .... 19 -- ....

Subject .... Duty Report - 8th April 19-- ....

....

Officer Reporting .... Police Constable 427 .... R. WALDRON ....

To .. Ch/Supt. PARKHOUSE .... 'B' .... Division

Sir,

     I have been asked to submit a duty report concerning my actions, while on duty, between 7.30 p.m. and 9.30 p.m. on Tuesday, 8th April 19--.

     I would report that for the whole of that period I was on duty, in the enquiry office, at the CHELTENHAM Police Station.

     At no time did I receive any found property from any person, neither did I see any property handed in at the desk, during that time.

     Also working in the enquiry office during that time, were Police Sergeant WALTERS and Mr YOUNG, the civilian clerk.

Police Constable No. 427

There are infrequent occasions when you will be requested to submit a **duty report**. It could be required because something has occurred on your beat and your knowledge of it or action concerning it, is in question. It could also be in connection with a disciplinary enquiry.

A request for such a report always contains details of the precise information required. Such a report is always submitted to your Divisional Commander.

The example given shows the usual format for such reports. It must be stressed that during your service you will encounter this report only rarely but you need to be aware of its existence.

Simple offence report

This is usually in the form of a booklet or pro-forma, containing both a self-explanatory section and provision for an offence statement.

When submitting reports on simple offences, usually to do with traffic violations, a **simple offence report** is completed. Although all the forces in England and Wales have individually designed booklets or pro-formas, which are used on these occasions, all of the varying designs will have two common factors.

First, each booklet or pro-forma will have a self-explanatory section which is simplicity itself to complete, usually by recording personal details of the offender/driving documents/administrative minutae.

The second section is completed by the composition of an offence statement containing the factual detail plus the offence detail. With the teaching you have received in Chapters 2 and 3 you are now in a position to complete such a simple offence report.

Those then are the four simple reports used by police officers. With your knowledge of statement construction, necessary only with the simple offence report, you will have no problems in using any of these simplest of reports.

Full Reports

Although it is not intended to look in depth at **full reports** in this chapter, you need to know of them and their individual functions. There are four types of full report and they are as follows:

Occurrence report

An occurrence report concerning a non-offence incident. It can be, and often is, accompanied by statements.

You will remember, in Chapter 2, being introduced to an **occurrence statement** concerning an accident where a man fell from a ladder. In that particular instance the statement that was taken would be attached to a short **occurrence report** and then submitted to the Chief Superintendent, for the possible use of the Coroner.

Although statements need not necessarily be taken to accompany an occurrence report, in this and most instances they would be taken. Chapter 6 deals in depth with both this and the following type of report.

Foreign station enquiry report

A report concerning an incident, requesting specified action, by an officer at a station other than the station from which the report originates.

With the criminal travelling far afield these days and the public moving more easily around the country for holidays, education and employment, you will find that often in order to complete an enquiry someone needs to be seen who is not currently within your district or force area. In order for that enquiry to be completed you will be required to submit a **foreign station enquiry report**. The definition of this report is self-explanatory.

Process report file

A report accompanied by statements and other documents for the intended presentation of a prosecution at a Magistrates' or Crown Court.

This type of report is completed for the more serious of offences involving crime, serious accidents or prosecutions for careless or reckless driving. The decision maker in such cases is the Crown Prosecution Service.

The three specimen reports in Part 2 are all full reports and come within this classification. Chapter 5 deals almost exclusively with the construction of this most common of full reports.

Reports to the Director of Public Prosecutions

A process report — requiring the approval of the Director of Public Prosecutions to prosecute — prepared and presented in a manner laid down by the Director.

There are some offences which still require the consent of the DPP before a prosecution can be commenced. A certain style and format has been laid down by the Director as to how these reports are to be prepared and although this book does not teach the construction of this type of report, you should know that the teaching on report writing as a whole is designed, very much, with the advice of the Director in mind. Once you have mastered the methods taught in this book you will find little difficulty in compiling reports to the highest standard, including **reports to the DPP**.

The eight types of report set out in this chapter are the only types you will encounter throughout your service. How then do you use the differing types of report and how best to prepare yourself?

As with the skill of statement writing, where a simple method of approach was suggested, so with this second skill of report construction there is a reliable basis from which to work, referred to as **thinking it through**.

Thinking it through

1. 'What is the information I have?'
2. 'Who is the decision maker?'
3. 'What decision am I asking him to make?'
4. 'What information does he need to make that decision?'

When considering the type, style and content of a report, the officer should ask himself four questions.

1. 'What is the information I have?'
2. 'Who is the decision maker?'
3. 'What decision am I asking him to make?'
4. 'What information does he need to make that decision?'

By using this thinking it through method you will naturally choose the correct type of report from the eight types available and, further, you will automatically begin to plan and design the content of your report almost without realising it.

In order to illustrate this process, consider the four questions individually applied to the four very different incidents portrayed in the illustration, namely: (a) a sudden death; (b) failing to comply with a red traffic light; (c) application for rent allowance; (d) grievous bodily harm.

1. *'What is the information I have?'* With this question you are classifying the information, fitting it in to one of the eight types of report which will properly convey the information thus:

(a) Sudden death	Occurrence report
(b) Fail to comply	Simple offence report
(c) Application for rent allowance	Administrative report
(d) Grievous bodily harm	Process report file

2. *'Who is the decision maker?'* This question will quickly follow the first and equally quickly be answered as follows:

(a) Sudden death	Coroner/Div. Commander
(b) Fail to comply	Sub-divisional officer
(c) Application for rent allowance	Civilian administrator
(d) Grievous bodily harm	Crown Prosecution Service

3. *'What decision am I asking him to make?'* The first two questions are simple, concerned only with classifying the report and identifying the decision maker. By trying to answer this third question and the following one, you are now beginning to *think through for yourself* the method of construction and required content of your proposed report.

(a) Sudden death	The cause of death
(b) Fail to comply	Whether to issue a summons
(c) Application for rent allowance	Whether I qualify for rent allowance
(d) Grievous bodily harm	Whether to charge or not

4. *'What information does he need to make that decision?'* This final question is the key to the whole process. As an operational officer you now apply your mind to working out exactly *what* the particular decision maker requires *from you* then ensure that it is in your report. In relation to the sudden death and the grievous bodily harm incidents, do not concern yourself with how that detail is conveyed to the decision maker, that will be covered in the next two chapters. All you have to do at this stage is work out what it is that he or she needs.

(a) Sudden death:
     Time, day, date and place of death. Relevant personal and medical details of deceased. Circumstances of death. Witnesses, proof of death and post-mortem result.
(b) Fail to comply:
     Factual detail *plus* offence detail.
(c) Application for rent allowance:
     All the qualifications (if they exist) required for payment of the allowance.
(d) Grievous bodily harm:
     Factual detail plus offence detail/opinion/hearsay/relevant facts in addition to points to prove/defences/other matters, e.g. previous convictions, further enquiries that need to be made.

You should see now how these four simple questions in thinking it through marshall your thoughts, make you aware of *what* it is you are trying to achieve with your report and *how* to attain it. It really is that simple.

Thought it through

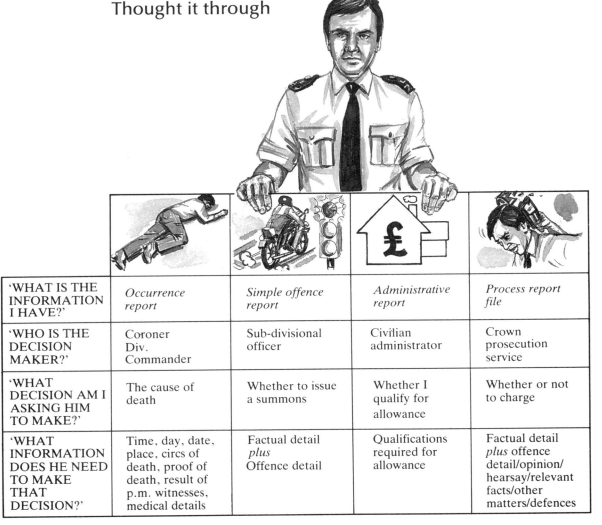

'WHAT IS THE INFORMATION I HAVE?'	*Occurrence report*	*Simple offence report*	*Administrative report*	*Process report file*
'WHO IS THE DECISION MAKER?'	Coroner Div. Commander	Sub-divisional officer	Civilian administrator	Crown prosecution service
'WHAT DECISION AM I ASKING HIM TO MAKE?'	The cause of death	Whether to issue a summons	Whether I qualify for allowance	Whether or not to charge
'WHAT INFORMATION DOES HE NEED TO MAKE THAT DECISION?'	Time, day, date, place, circs of death, proof of death, result of p.m. witnesses, medical details	Factual detail *plus* Offence detail	Qualifications required for allowance	Factual detail *plus* offence detail/opinion/ hearsay/relevant facts/other matters/defences

Procedural rules

In relation to *all* reports the following rules apply:

1. Whoever the decision maker, *all* reports are addressed to the Divisional Chief Superintendent and commence with the word 'Sir'.
2. Surnames and place names are printed in BLOCK CAPITALS.
3. *All* reports are signed by the officer submitting together with his rank and number.

These rules have been kept to a minimum. Rules (1) and (3) above are already standard practice in most of the forces in England and Wales while rule (2) reinforces a statement writing rule you encountered in Chapter 2.

Conclusion

This chapter has been important for two main reasons.

First you have learned of the eight differing types of report used in police work.

Second, you have been shown a simple thought process by the use of which the correct type of report will be selected. Further, that same thought process guides you through the construction of whatever report has been selected.

The next two chapters build on these two important pieces of learning.

5 Full report construction

Before continuing with this chapter it is suggested that you familiarise yourself with the statements, the contemporaneous notes of interview and other miscellaneous documents contained in Report A, the shoplifting case.

In addition you should refresh your memory on the *purpose of a report* (page 44) and consider again the thought process triggered by the four questions in 'Thinking it through' (page 49).

The following points in connection with report construction are covered in this chapter:

1. The three simple sections which make up a full report.
2. An examination in detail of those three sections, namely: the main heading; the summary; and other matters.
3. Some simple directions or 'Good habits' which will assist you in writing your reports.

Building a case

Whether the offence is simple or complex, when dealing with a suspected offender you, as an operational police offender, *build a case* against that person, if it exists.

With almost all summary offences you require only *factual detail* plus *offence detail* to be present and your building process is complete. A simple offence report is all that is required. The compilation of such a simple report has already been described in Chapter 4.

With criminal offences or the more serious traffic violations in order to build your case you will require other additional points to be present. These 'add-ons' were outlined in Chapter 3.

Well-constructed reports, therefore, not only meet the requirements of Questions 3 and 4 of 'Thinking it through' (page 49) but also illustrate to the decision maker how well you have built your case. Full reports demonstrate this building process extremely well and none more so than the process report file.

Of the eight types of report used in police work, the full report is the one which appears to cause most problems, not only to the person compiling but also to the person to whom it is submitted. If the teaching in this chapter is followed by compiler and receiver alike, then those problems should vanish.

Although this chapter is concerned with the construction of a **process report file** you will find that mastery of the teaching within this chapter makes the next chapter, concerned with **occurrence reports** and **foreign station enquiry reports**, simplicity itself. In other words this chapter, coupled with Chapter 4, really is the key to good report construction.

The construction of a process report file

Using the statements and other documents contained in Report A let us together answer the four questions from 'Thinking it through' as follows:

1. *'What is the information I have?'* This question, you will remember, is answered by classifying the information you have and selecting one of the eight types of report. From the statements within the specimen report you should be able to decide that this is a case which involves theft of property, therefore a **process report file** is required.

2. *'Who is the decision maker?'* The decision maker is the **Crown Prosecution Service**, although your report will be addressed to the Chief Superintendent of your Division.

3. *'What is the decision I am asking him to make?'* The decision in this case, as with most cases, is *whether or not to charge the alleged offender*. In practice you will often find that a person will be charged and then a file will be compiled and submitted to the Crown Prosecution Service (CPS) who confirm, or otherwise, that process should continue.

4. *'What information does he need to make a decision?'* The answer to this question has already been given in Chapter 4 and you should remember that it is **Factual detail plus offence detail/opinion/hearsay/relevant facts in addition to points to prove/defences/other matters.**

How then, in answer to Questions 3 and 4 above, is that information presented to the decision maker in a process report file? First, you need to know what constitutes a full report.

The content of a full report

The format for *all* reports is governed by the content and this can be divided into three simple sections:

1. The main heading.
2. The summary.
3. Other matters.

Building a case

Together we shall look now at these three sections, individually and in detail, and see how they are applied to the shoplifting case.

1. The main heading
This consists of:

(a) Full personal details of the alleged offender.
(b) The charges (preferred or intended).
(c) Full list of witnesses.
(d) List of exhibits.

Applying this definition to the 'shoplifting' case, see, in the following example, how *all* the detail conveyed to the decision maker in the **main heading** (with the exception of the charge) comprises of '..*information drawn from statements..*' *which, you will remember, is one of the purposes of a report.*

WHO —	OFFENDER	LOCKE,	Patricia Mary 13 Mile End Causeway BRISTOL born 03.05.44 Housewife

WHAT — SUGGESTED CHARGE At BRISTOL in the County of Avon, on 3rd February 19 – – , stole two pieces of meat to the total value of £7.55, the property of Oxenbury's Foodstore Ltd.

Contrary to Section 1 Theft Act 1968

HOW — WITNESSES

1. COOPER, Ian Jonathon
Store Detective
71 Westway Road
Fishponds BRISTOL

2. WILLS, Kenneth George
Store Manager
The Old Rectory
Stoke Gifford
BRISTOL

3. LEWIS, Heather
Nurse
3 Hilly Gardens Road
Fishponds BRISTOL

4. REDMORE, Ian
Detective Constable 556
Avon and Somerset
Constabulary
Fishponds BRISTOL

5. TAYLOR, Paul Stephen
Detective Constable 1671
Avon and Somerset
Constabulary
Fishponds BRISTOL

EXHIBITS

1. Green plastic bag	ST/1
2. One piece of steak	ST/2
3. One piece of steak	ST/3
4. One till roll	ST/4
5. Contemporaneous notes	IR/1

The main heading informs the decision maker, in three simple steps:

Who is alleged to have done
What and
How it is proved.

Most forces in England and Wales have their own individually designed forms for the main heading but you will find that they are, all of them, based upon this simple format, which you have now learned.

Two small procedural points are worth noting.

1. Where a person has been charged with an offence the main heading will include the words 'stands charged', whereas if the person has not been charged the words 'suggested charge' will be used.
2. Police officers are generally placed at the end of the list of witnesses with the reporting officer listed last.

2. The summary
This consists of:
(a) A brief introduction.
(b) A précis of the evidence.

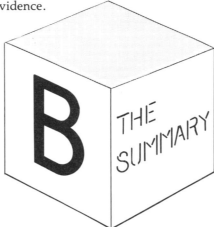

This is the part of report writing which seems to cause problems for many officers but, once mastered, it is the part that will bring you the most satisfaction.

Before composing the **summary** for our 'shoplifting' case let me give you a worthwhile, practical hint, applicable to *all* of the cases that lie ahead of you.

It is sound practice, when you are preparing to construct the summary, to sit down with the statements and any other relevant documents and rough out the points you consider to be significant or worthy of special note. This applies not only to admissible evidence but also to any other fact which you think pertinent.

By doing so you are then collecting and directing your thoughts in a systematic and disciplined manner and you will find that your case will build (or not) before your very eyes.

Let us now consider the 'shoplifting' case and begin our summary with the following:

(a) **A brief introduction** This, in effect, is a paragraph or paragraphs, outlining the allegation(s). It is, as it says, the briefest of digests of the incident.

It is strange but it is a fact that actually to start a report is often, for some officers, the most difficult step in report writing. This difficulty is removed by using the recommended start to the introduction, which is the phrase, 'This report concerns...' followed by the brief digest of the incident.

Brief introduction — This report concerns the alleged theft, by the above named LOCKE, of two pieces of meat, total value £7.55, from Oxenbury's Food Store at FISHPONDS on 3rd February 19——. Briefly the facts are as follows:

A recommended ending to the introduction is the phrase 'Briefly the facts are as follows'. This phrase naturally leads the writer and the reader on to the next section of the summary.

(b) **A précis of the evidence** In order to achieve a concise, relevant précis of the evidence you will need to scan each statement and then *briefly* highlight the more important and pertinent points of that statement. You are actually building your case for the decision maker and drawing attention to the information needed to make a decision.

When considering what to include in your *précis*, that which bests assists the decision maker, you need to go no further than to include:

(i) Factual detail plus offence detail.
(ii) Additional facts (admissible or non-admissible).

Get into the habit of distilling the important points from each statement into one or two paragraphs. Consider, for example, the three-page statement of COOPER (pages 116−118) and see how, in two short paragraphs, the decision maker is presented with the primary evidence from this witness. Note also how the first of these paragraphs illustrates the inclusion of factual detail and offence detail.

Factual detail	At about 10.45 a.m. that day, the Accused was seen to enter the store by the store detective, the witness COOPER. He kept her under observation
Offence detail (appropriates property)	throughout the whole of the time she was in the store and saw her select a number of items from the display shelves, including the two pieces of steak. When LOCKE came to the check-out, COOPER noted that she failed to produce or pay for the two pieces of steak, he had earlier seen her select.
Accused's conduct	Outside the store, he challenged LOCKE, who denied the theft, but agreed to accompany COOPER to the manager's office.

The independent civilian witness LEWIS actually saw the theft take place. Her statement has been condensed to four lines, which emphasise this important evidence. This witness tends to prove that the Accused acted 'dishonestly', vital offence detail.

Supportive offence detail (dishonestly)	The witness LEWIS was in the store at the time and actually saw the Accused place the stolen items into a plastic carrier bag (ST/1), instead of the wire basket, provided by the store.

The next witness is Detective Constable TAYLOR and because he is the officer submitting the report, he refers to himself as 'the reporting officer'.

Note how his evidence of the important happenings at the store is condensed into six lines.

Supportive offence detail/ exhibits	The reporting officer attended and in the store manager's office, in the presence of the Accused, searched the plastic bag and found the two pieces of steak (ST/2 and 3), together with a till roll (ST/4), which clearly showed she had not paid for the meat.

The next paragraph neatly dovetails the supporting evidence of WILLS, the store manager, with that of COOPER, showing the recovery of the stolen property and the fact that it belonged to the store, again important offence detail.

Supportive offence detail (belonging to another)	The manager of the store, the witness WILLS, supports the evidence of the brief interview of the Accused and the search which took place in his office, as does the witness COOPER. Further, WILLS gives evidence as to ownership and value of the stolen items.

The final paragraph of the summary covers the arrest and removal of the Accused to a police station, her interview and admission of guilt (offence detail), and the fact that D.C. REDMORE took down and produces the contemporaneous notes of interview. All this detail, contained in five short lines.

Offence detail/ exhibit (permanently deprive)	The Accused was arrested and taken to the Fishponds Police Station, where later, when interviewed, she made a full admission, details of which appear in the contemporaneous note of the interview (IR/1), taken by Detective Constable REDMORE.

Seven comparatively short paragraphs have been used to outline to the decision maker how the case has been built up or proved, all condensed from 14 pages of statement and interview notes.

This summary, and yours, should be a concise, relevant précis of the statements which build your case. I make no apology for repeating that the summary is a précis of the statements. Remember *reports are never duplicates of statements.*

Although, of course, the decision maker will read the statements, the summary should set out exactly, yet concisely, what it is that is alleged against the Accused. Each paragraph, though packed with information should be spare and economical, as in the examples above. I would commend this style of report writing to you.

3. Other matters

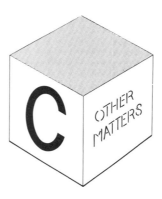

This is an area of the report where you, as the reporting officer, can include anything you consider to be relevant. Having said that, you should not indulge yourself aimlessly. Brevity and clarity should remain your aims.

Although you can include anything you consider to be relevant there are a number of headings which cover the more common subjects usually dealt with in this part of the report.

(a) *Previous convictions of the Accused.* Always carry out a PNC check on your suspect and note in **other matters** whether or not there are any previous convictions. A copy of the PNC printout should be attached to the report where there are previous convictions.

(b) *Reliability, previous history, personal details of witness.* Often it is necessary to remark on the reliability or worth of witnesses or their relationship with the Accused. Whether for or against the Accused, if such facts are likely to affect a case you should inform the decision maker.

(c) *Other enquiries/offences/relevant facts involving the Accused.* The Accused may be the subject of suspicion for, or may wish to admit, other offences. Anything concerning the Accused, be it favourable or damning, should be noted here.

(d) *Recommendations/requests, if applicable, of the reporting officer.* If you, as the officer in the case, feel strongly about some feature of the case, then you should say so. This is the opportunity for you to speak directly to the decision maker. I do not suggest that you continually put a recommendation on all your reports, but the facility exists, so use it, but again be brief and relevant.

(e) *The current position concerning the Accused (whether charged/in custody/on bail/court appearances).* Time is important, particularly the time a person spends in custody prior to trial. It follows, therefore, that the decision maker should be fully aware of the *current position concerning the Accused.*

'Other matters' in this, our report on the shoplifting case, has three paragraphs.

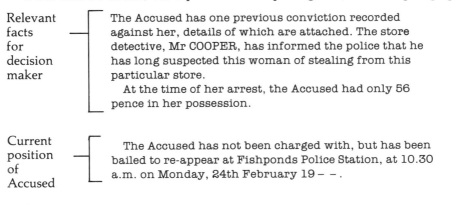

Relevant facts for decision maker — The Accused has one previous conviction recorded against her, details of which are attached. The store detective, Mr COOPER, has informed the police that he has long suspected this woman of stealing from this particular store.

At the time of her arrest, the Accused had only 56 pence in her possession.

Current position of Accused — The Accused has not been charged with, but has been bailed to re-appear at Fishponds Police Station, at 10.30 a.m. on Monday, 24th February 19 – –.

Detective Constable 1671

The three important facts outlined in the first two paragraphs are all gleaned from the documents found on pages 130 – 132.

The Accused's previous convictions are relevant and should be attached to the report itself. The store detective's suspicions, though not admissible, should be brought to the attention of the decision maker, while the fact that the Accused had only 56 pence in her possession shows an inability to pay for the stolen item (*relevant facts involving the Accused*).

The final paragraph shows the current position of the Accused.

Those then are the three parts of a process report file. You will find, if you approach all your cases by dividing your report into these three sections, that report writing will cease to be a problem.

You will discover after two or three attempts that you will automatically divide and structure your report under the three headings and, working to this simple system, the report will naturally flow.

Good Habits

1. *Collect and direct your thoughts by preparation.* I have already mentioned this 'good habit' previously in the chapter. Good preparation is essential whatever the size of report you are compiling. Lack of preparation invariably means a poor report and a failure by you to represent properly the public.

2. *Content is decided by:*

   (a) Factual detail plus offence detail.
   (b) Thinking it through.

   As you have seen in the compilation of the report on the shoplifting case, the content of a report is not an aimless meandering through disconnected facts. By applying the details from the jigsaw and considering the questions from 'Thinking it through', you will naturally find the correct content for all your reports.

3. *Reports are read from front to back.* Although this may be an obvious fact to state, what it should mean to you is that the decision maker reads your reports from the front to the back, therefore it is essential he knows, as early as possible *who* has done *what* and *how* it is proved. The format and style you have learned in this chapter achieve just that.

4. *Reports are never duplicates of statements.* Again this fact has been previously highlighted but it is well worth repeating. Your skill in report writing is really the skill of distilling from statements those important facts of which a decision maker needs to be aware. By applying point (2) above you can easily achieve this.

5. *Always be clear, relevant and concise.* Throughout this chapter the need for your report writing to be clear, relevant and concise has been continually stressed.

Improving your skills

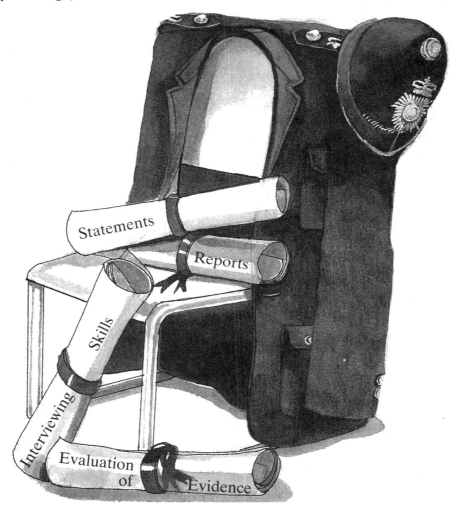

The three full reports in Part 2 contain a number of useful examples of the techniques of report construction.

1. Accident report (page 135) **10

In this report see how the reporting officer has packed into the 'brief introduction' almost all the details concerning the time, day, date, place and vehicles involved. All this within five short lines.

2. Accident report (page 135) **11

The fourth paragraph of this report records the admission by the defendant to the witness RELPH that he has been at fault. Note that there is no requirement to quote, in the report, the direct speech used. However, if you wish to insert a quote, you can.

3. Assault report (page 159) **12
   Again the 'brief introduction' in this report has encapsulated all the relevant detail about this case and, in addition, has captured the interest of the reader. It is a short (seven lines) and impactive start to a report.

4. Assault report (page 159) **13
   Note how in the fourth paragraph of this report the reporting officer has neatly summarised the seven pages of evidence from the two witnesses OAKDEN and GRIGG, with a five-line paragraph. Just a few words, if correctly chosen, can convey much detail.

5. Assault report (page 159) **14
   The penultimate paragraph of the report outlining the details of the alleged offender's previous convictions is most pertinent, drawing attention, as it does, to the previous use of weapons.

6

Occurrence and foreign station enquiry reports

This chapter deals with the construction of two important types of full report, namely **occurrence reports** and **foreign station enquiry reports**.

There are no new principles, definitions or procedures for you to learn. Chapters 4 and 5 have equipped you with sufficient skill to prepare both reports.

An occurrence report

A report concerning a non-offence incident, it can be, and often is, accompanied by statements.

Incidents such as sudden deaths, road defects, domestic disputes or accidents/illness in the street are of the type where an occurrence report is used. In order to illustrate the construction of this report we shall, together, look again at the incident involving the man falling from the ladder, described in Chapter 2 and about which an **occurrence statement** was made by the witness Phillip James HARDCASTLE (page 22).

Three other persons, Edwin JOHNS, William PERKINS and James COLLINS were all witnesses to some of the circumstances surrounding this incident and their occurrence statements appear on pages 187 to 192. You should read those four statements before continuing further.

Now, armed with the information you have gathered from the statements, how would you set about compiling an occurrence report to accompany them? Of course the application of *thinking it through* as a first step in the preparation of the report should be very familiar to you now. It is as follows:

1. *'What is the information I have?'* This is obviously a non-offence incident therefore such a classification demands the preparation of an *occurrence report*.
2. *'Who is the decision maker?'* With the facts as they stand (a person seriously injured, but still alive) then the decision maker is the Divisional Chief Superintendent. However, if the man subsequently died then the decision maker would be HM Coroner.
3. *'What decision am I asking him to make?'* Although occurrence reports are primarily of an informative nature, the decision in this instance is whether or not this was an *accidental fall*.
4. *'What information does he need to make that decision?'* The decision maker needs to be acquainted with those facts which illustrate the incident well but, in addition, show that it was an accidental fall.

Having answered the four questions of the thinking it through process how then to construct an occurrence report concerning this accident in the street?

You have already learned that the content of a full report is divided into three simple sections, namely:

— The main heading.
— The summary.
— Other matters.

As only **process report files** and **reports to the DPP** deal with offence incidents then only those two types of *full report* need to illustrate to the decision maker *who* has done *what* and *how* it is proved. The main heading therefore is not required in an occurrence report, which commences, straight away, with the summary. It consists of:

A brief introduction

As in the process report file, this is the briefest of digests introducing the decision maker to the incident.

> 'This report concerns an industrial accident, which occurred at about 12.30 p.m. on Friday, 1st July 19 — —, in Fore Street, ST IVES, when Colin PENBERTHY, fell from scaffolding, on to the ground and received serious injuries. Briefly the facts are as follows:'

You will see, from the above, that the standard opening 'This report concerns...' has been used, as has the equally standard closing phrase, 'Briefly the facts are as follows...'. By using these simple, short phrases you will find, with practice, that the report almost writes itself.

A précis of the evidence

As you have already learned, in Chapter 2, occurrence statements are not necessarily concerned with evidence, in the strictest sense of the word. Similarly occurrence reports, covering non-offence incidents obviously do not contain either factual detail or offence detail. However, the same system of distilling the relevant details from the statements, for the information of the decision maker, is employed.

The statement of the witness JOHNS has been scanned and a four-paragraph précis has been made, as follows:

> 'During the past two weeks, Mr Edwin JOHNS, building contractor of No.2 Back Road West, ST IVES, has been carrying out repair work to the front and roof of CURNOWS' gift shop, Fore Street, ST IVES.
>
> Three of his workmen, including PENBERTHY, have been employed on that work and, in order to carry out such work, scaffolding has had to be erected outside the shop, to a height of some 30 feet. All materials and waste have had to be carried by hand, and this includes the removal of a large number of tiles from the roof.
>
> Mr JOHNS has warned his men not to attempt to carry too much, when conveying materials and had to remind PENBERTHY of this precaution, as recently as Thursday, 30th June 19 — —.
>
> At about 12.10 p.m. on Friday, 1st July 19 — —, JOHNS left the site and upon his return, some 15 or 20 minutes later, found that PENBERTHY had fallen off the scaffolding, while carrying a load of slates.'

Note how the précis of this witness's statement has been used to set out the background and circumstances leading up to the accident and, although the other two workmen from the firm give the same information, when a précis of their statements is made this background information is not then included.

Observe, however, that what is stressed, is the *probable cause* of the accident and both workmen comment, in their separate ways, on this fact. First the witness PERKINS:

> 'The two other men working at the site, both tell of PENBERTHY attempting to carry more than was thought to be safe.
>
> William PERKINS, a labourer of 3 Digey Cottages, The Stennack, ST IVES confirms that JOHNS gave advice concerning safety and states that just before the accident PENBERTHY told him of his intention to carry more than the suggested number of tiles.'

The witness COLLINS supports the previous witness:

> 'James COLLINS, a labourer of 2 Coastguard Cottages, ST IVES also confirms that immediately prior to the accident PENBERTHY stated his intention to carry a large number of tiles. COLLINS further tells of a conversation PENBERTHY had with a female holiday maker in which he [PENBERTHY] boasted about how easy it was to carry such loads.'

The independent witness HARDCASTLE saw the fall and all-important fact that PENBERTHY appeared to be carrying too many tiles. These relevant facts from his statement have been presented in six lines, as follows:

'Mr Phillip HARDCASTLE, a holiday maker, of No. 50 Otley Road, LEEDS, Yorkshire describes having his attention drawn to the accident by his wife Angela. Mr HARDCASTLE actually saw PENBERTHY fall and can say that, at the time, he [PENBERTHY] was attempting to carry a load of slates.'

Within eight short paragraphs the decision maker has been made aware of the main points drawn from the fourteen pages of statements.

Other Matters

In Chapter 5 you were told that '...this section can include anything considered relevant...' and in particular '...the current position concerning the Accused...'.

With occurrence reports there is no Accused, but invariably there is a person or persons who are the subject of the report. In this instance it is the man PENBERTHY. It is only right to include in the report, therefore, '...the current position concerning the [subject]...'. This is achieved as follows:

'PENBERTHY was taken to the Edward Hain Hospital, at ST IVES where an X-ray examination, on admission, revealed that he had fractured his skull.

PENBERTHY remains stable, though unconscious and his condition is described as critical. It is too early, at this stage, for medical experts to fully diagnose PENBERTHY's condition, accordingly a statement, as yet, has not been obtained from the hospital staff.

This report is submitted for your information to be retained for use by the Coroner, if required.'

The final two-line paragraph neatly comes under the heading of '...recommendations...' in that the reporting officer submitting this report has explained why he has submitted the report (and statements) and what possible use they might, in the future, serve.

A straightforward report construction, I think you will agree, of the second of the four types of full report. Note, however, that although this is a totally different incident being reported on, as compared to the shoplifting case, the same logical system is used in the construction process.

The second part of this chapter deals with a report you were briefly introduced to in Chapter 2.

A foreign station enquiry report

A report concerning an incident, requesting specified action, by an officer at a station other than the station from which the report originates.

Regularly there will be occasions when you require action to be taken, in connection with an investigation, at a place not within your own area. This action may not warrant sending either you or a fellow officer from your station to carry out that enquiry. In such an instance a **foreign station enquiry report** is prepared.

Yet again, although this is one of the four *full* reports, its method of construction is simplicity itself. In order to illustrate how such a report is constructed I intend to return again to the accident involving the man PENBERTHY, falling from the ladder.

You will recall that the witness HARDCASTLE, who was on holiday in Cornwall, was from Yorkshire and was accompanied by his wife Angela. From the statements you have already seen you will know that she is alleged to have seen the accident and had, apparently, been talking to PENBERTHY prior to his fall.

For the purpose of illustration let us suppose that you have decided that Angela HARDCASTLE needs to be interviewed and that if possible she should make a written statement concerning the following:

—   All she can say about the incident.
—   In particular was she the woman talking to PENBERTHY?
—   If so, what was said?
—   What estimate can she give as to the number of slates being carried by PENBERTHY?

Armed with the information from the four statements, how is the foreign station enquiry report to be constructed? As always, with any report, you start with the four questions from 'Thinking it through'.

1.   *'What is the information I have?'* The information you have concerns a non-offence incident and you wish action to be taken on that information by another officer. Therefore, the answer to this 'classifying' question is a foreign station enquiry report.
2.   *'Who is the decision maker?'* The decision maker will be your *Divisional Chief Superintendent* or his deputy.
3.   *'What decision am I asking him to make?'* The decision you are asking of the Chief Superintendent is *whether the report should be sent and the action you request, taken.*
4.   *'What information does he need to make that decision?'* You need to be aware that the report will, hopefully, be sent to and read by another officer, at another station, who will act on your behalf. Therefore, in answer to this question, the report needs to be so worded that:
   (a)   it satisfies the Chief Superintendent; and
   (b)   is so informative that the police officer, at the other station, who is to carry out the enquiry, knows exactly what is required of him.

The fact that this is a kind of dual purpose report in no way makes it any more difficult to write, as I shall now illustrate.

The brief introduction

This is a non-offence incident so here again there is no need for a *main heading*. The report starts therefore with *the summary*, the first part of which is the *brief introduction*. Note how the phrase 'This report concerns...' introduces not only a précis of the incident, but also informs the decision maker that there is a request for further police action. All this within six lines.

> 'This report concerns a request for further police enquiries in connection with an industrial accident which occurred in Fore Street, ST IVES when a local man, Colin PENBERTHY, fell from scaffolding on to the ground and received injuries.
> PENBERTHY has failed to regain consciousness and is currently on the critical list.'

A précis of the evidence

In such a report as this you are:

1. Trying to justify to the Divisional Commander a course of action (in this instance the interviewing of a witness). The précis, therefore, should reflect the facts which justify this action.
2. Asking yourself 'What does *he* or *she...*', in this case the other officer, '...need to know' in order to carry out the enquiry. You will be suprised how simply both these objectives can be achieved at the same time, as follows:

> 'A number of persons witnessed this accident, including a Mr Phillip HARDCASTLE, of 50 Otley Road, LEEDS, Yorkshire, who was on holiday in ST IVES, at the time, but has since returned to LEEDS.
> He was accompanied by his wife Angela, who, it is thought, witnessed this accident, and more importantly, the events leading up to it.
> James COLLINS, another witness at the scene, describes the injured man, talking to a female holiday maker, thought to be Mrs Angela HARDCASTLE.
> The statements of COLLINS and HARDCASTLE are attached.'

I think you will agree that the needs of the Divisional Chief Superintendent and the other officer who is to carry out the enquiry are both satisfied by the above four paragraphs.

Notice how I have referred within the précis to only two of the witnesses and have not mentioned JOHNS or PERKINS. In my opinion neither of these two latter witnesses give relevant information concerning Angela HARDCASTLE, hence I have excluded them. I do not consider that they would assist the officer making the enquiry on my behalf. This is a matter of opinion and you may disagree.

Other matters

Having described the incident in the *brief introduction* and set out the circumstances in the *précis of the evidence*, the final part of the report sets out *other matters*, which in this case are '...requests of the reporting officer...'

'I ask that an officer interview Mrs HARDCASTLE in connection with this incident and take a statement from her and that the following points in particular, be covered in that statement.

(a) Was she the woman to whom PENBERTHY spoke, as described in the statement from COLLINS?

(b) If so, what did PENBERTHY say to her?

(c) Can she give any estimate of the number of tiles being carried by PENBERTHY immediately before his fall?

I ask that this report and the attached statements be forwarded to the Chief Officer of Police, West Yorkshire Constabulary, LEEDS, Yorkshire, in order that an officer may carry out this enquiry.'

That is all you need to know about the construction of an occurrence report and a foreign station enquiry report. You should now be able to see that by continually applying the simple basic procedures outlined in this and the two preceeding chapters, good report writing is simply a matter of practice.

The compilation of *all* full reports, including that of a DPP file, is based upon a simple step-by-step construction process *plus* the ability to extract from statements and other documents the relevant details and present them in a concise, clear manner.

You have now been taught the step-by-step construction procedure and, by applying it, you will find that your ability to extract and present the relevant information will be improved.

Having dealt with statement writing and report construction you have now covered two of the four police skills. This is an ideal point at which to stop and take stock. You should be able to see how the skills are beginning to interlink, one with the other, with much of the teaching on statements being most relevant to report construction.

Remember how, in the very first instant at the scene of an incident, the four questions in the 'Method of approach' naturally led you on to the jigsaw design which, in turn, correctly directed your thoughts to the content of an offence statement. In addition, you later learned of the important additional factors which are grafted on to the jigsaw design in the more complex of statements.

Report construction relied heavily on the teaching you had already been given concerning statements and here again your thoughts were properly channelled by answering the four questions in 'Thinking it through' which, in turn, led you on to the three stages (the main heading, the summary and other matters) involved in 'building a case'.

Throughout it all ran the common thread of factual detail plus offence detail epitomised in this book by the jigsaw design and upon which the whole book is based.

The next two chapters cover the skills of interviewing and evaluating evidence and increasingly you will see how the system you have already been taught continues to be applied.

Believe it or not you are now genuinely in a position to tackle both of these two important skills, virtually by simply applying what you have already been shown. The next two chapters will show you how.

Improving your skills

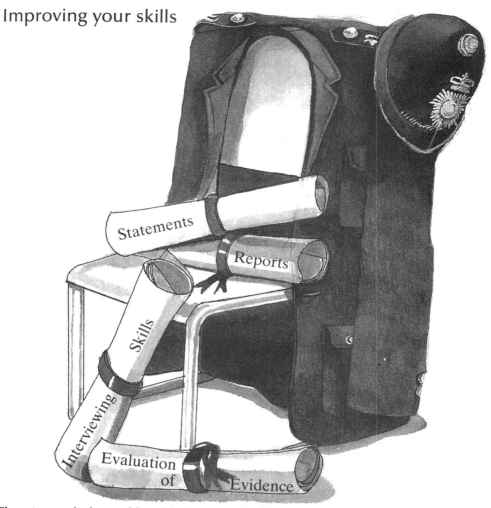

There is very little to add to this chapter, which might be of assistance to you, except the following three points.

1. Note how, with the foreign station enquiry report, I dispatched copies of the statements of COLLINS and HARDCASTLE. This is a good habit as it means that the report is kept comparatively short and, further, the officer making the enquiry has, to hand, the statements relevant to his or her enquiry, for possible unforeseen queries.

2. If the preceding point is applicable, then it goes without saying that it is imperative you display your skill in properly condensing the pertinent points of the statements which are to accompany the report. Remember, however simple or short a report may be, always maintain the highest of standards in its construction.

3. I have included in Part 2, on pages 193 — 196, both the occurrence report and the foreign station enquiry report in their finished state. They are amazingly similar and, if it were possible to do so, the inclusion of a main heading would make both virtually indistinguishable from a process report file. This should illustrate to you the flexibility of the system you are being taught.

7

Interviewing skill

This chapter deals with the important police skill of interviewing. It covers the following points:

1. The concept, content of and reason for a police interview.
2. Some preparatory steps taken before a police interview.
3. Simple guidelines for use when conducting a police interview.

Can I stress, first of all, that this chapter is *not* concerned with extracting confessions or conducting interrogations, but simply the **skill of interviewing**. Daily, police officers of all ranks conduct interviews, in respect of a myriad of incidents, and within this chapter such interviews are referred to as 'police' interviews.

Contrary to popular belief almost all good police interviews are conducted along the lines you will find described in this chapter. This applies equally to the relatively simple incidents such as the minor accident or crime as well as the more serious matters up to and including murder.

One of the interesting points of this chapter is that the content of *all* police interviews is built around the simple procedures you have already learned in the chapters on statement and report construction, It is in this chapter that you will see how one police skill is part of and naturally flows into the next. The true significance of the system you are learning will begin to take shape as this chapter unfolds.

A police interview

A police interview may be described as a meeting between a police officer and one or more persons in order that information may be obtained or exchanged.

This is a fairly self-explanatory definition and requires no further illumination from me except to state that such a definition applies to suspect and non-suspect alike. You will find, in fact, that, if properly conducted, there should be no differences in police interviews with either type of person.

The object of any police interview

The object of any police interview is to establish THE TRUTH, be it supportive or otherwise of an allegation or complaint.

Without, I hope, overstating the case, I would say that a number of basic principles, which underpin the character and style of policing in a liberal democracy, particularly in Britain, will emerge during this chapter. The most significant principle of them all, I would suggest, is the importance of *the truth*.

It could be said that, as police officers, you will naturally be 'prosecution minded'. In anticipation of a howl of protest I should further state that all organisations tend to instil in their members a particular way of thinking or of looking at things from a certain point of view. The police service is no exception.

Having said that, let me add that to be 'prosecution minded' is not necessarily an unhealthy attitude, particularly if a dispassionate, questioning approach is adopted. Neither need it be a dishonest way of looking at the world.

The quest, by you, for the truth, means that the facts will speak for themselves, whatever you think about them, and your attitude will have no bearing whatsoever on the outcome. The truth, therefore, is your safeguard against possible bias, '...be it supportive or otherwise of an allegation or complaint'.

Although the establishing of the truth is common to all police interviews, whether with suspect or non-suspect, there *are additional reasons for interviewing a suspect.*

Interviewing to represent the complainant

As I have previously stated, we, in the police service, are the representatives of the public, upholding for them the rule of law. It is from the public that the vast majority of complaints are received, although on occasions police officers themselves are the complainants. Whatever the case, in interviews with suspects the interviewing officer represents the complainant and acts on his behalf. The interview is the opportunity for the details of the complaint to be properly aired before any possible court hearing has been arranged.

Interviewing to acquaint the Accused/Defendant with the allegations

As well as safeguarding the rights of the complainant it is only proper that an Accused person should be treated fairly and made aware, *at the earliest date*, of any complaint or allegation made. The police interview is the occasion when this is achieved.

Interviewing to note properly any comment or explanation the Accused/Defendant may make

The crucial phrase in this paragraph is '...to note properly...'. You do not need to be told that when interviewing a suspect such an interview must be after caution. However, in addition, '...to note properly...' also means:

1. Notes made in a pocket notebook, *as soon as practicable* after the interview.
2. Contemporaneous verbatim notes taken of the interview.
3. A tape recording of the interview, taken under approved conditions

Preparing the ground for the interview

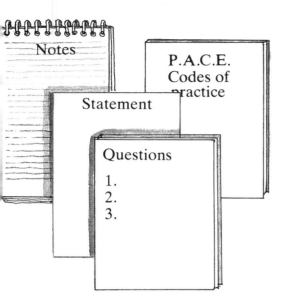

Preparation is the key to success in almost any task and, as we have already seen with statement and report construction, that is certainly true of police work. Accordingly, there are a number of fairly obvious steps which should, ideally, be completed before commencing an interview with a suspect or non-suspect.

1. *Ideally all enquiries that can be, should be completed particularly before interviews with suspected persons.* If possible, it is of prime importance that the interviewing officer be in possession of as many of the facts of the case as possible, before commencing an interview. This may seem an obvious fact, but it is suprising how many overlook the obvious.

2. *Be aware of the requirements of PACE.* There are a number of requirements under PACE which have to be complied with when conducting an interview. This book is not designed to teach the PACE Codes of Practice. As operational police officers you should be totally conversant with what is required of you and also aware of the fact that non-compliance with the Codes can make much good work inadmissible.

3. *When preparing for an interview, a written list of questions plus statements from persons who have witnessed the incident, can assist.* Basically, a police interview, can be divided into asking questions and noting replies. Therefore, it follows that you must know what questions it is you wish to ask. Preparing a list of questions serves two purposes. First of all it provides you with an *aide-mémoire*, but it also ensures that, in order to prepare such a list, you must have become fully conversant with all aspects of the case.

   Initially you may feel that using lists and referring to statements is a cumbersome method of interviewing. With continued practice, however, you will find that such aids become 'quick glance reminders' and, far from impeding the natural flow of a discussion, will actually help, giving you time to think and react to the information you are receiving during the interview.

Having covered the reasons for the preparation in respect of interviews, I would like now to move on to the actual skill of interviewing.

First a word of advice. You will find no mention in this book of the differing approaches to interviewing a violent person or one who is distressed, angry, antagonistic, helpful, afraid or in any other condition.

What this chapter sets out to achieve is to provide you with a rock solid system that will see you successfully through any interview, regardless of the approach of the other person.

Only by truly experiencing the differing moods of people in real-life situations, will you, personally, learn how to conduct yourself. You will find, however, that whatever the mood of the interview, the system you are learning will always work.

It is true to say that this chapter really is teaching you your craft as it is based very much on the tried and trusted methods and techniques used by experienced and successful police officers.

If you use these same methods and techniques then you truly are planning, thinking and working like a police officer.

The content of the interview

When interviewing any person, whether suspected or not, the following points should be covered, by the interviewing officer:

1. Method of approach.
2. Additional allegations.
3. Thinking it through.
4. Defences.
5. One more question.
6. Statement in writing.

For the purpose of illustration I intend to take you through two interviews in respect of the same road accident. The first interview will be with a non-offending driver, while the second interview is with the suspect.

First interview – the non-offending driver

You will see how, from the very first question, the police officer is working to a system that enables him to prepare an offence statement, based on the jigsaw template, as well as bearing in mind what he might need for his intended report, in compliance with the 'thinking it through' principle. In addition, and equally important, he or she is obtaining all the details required in order to interview the suspect. First, the interview with the non-suspect and a good point to bear in mind is that *the Accused is not present* when you are interviewing a witness so remember you are hearing only one side of the story.

1. Method of approach

Remember, in Chapter 2, how, at the scene of any incident you asked yourself the four questions *'What is this?'* *'Is it an offence?'*, *'What is the offence?'* and *'How do I prove the offence?'*.

The answer to the last question naturally takes you to the jigsaw template and factual detail plus offence detail, thus:

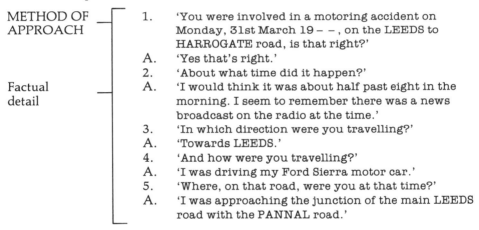

METHOD OF APPROACH

1. 'You were involved in a motoring accident on Monday, 31st March 19 – – , on the LEEDS to HARROGATE road, is that right?'
A. 'Yes that's right.'
2. 'About what time did it happen?'

Factual detail

A. 'I would think it was about half past eight in the morning. I seem to remember there was a news broadcast on the radio at the time.'
3. 'In which direction were you travelling?'
A. 'Towards LEEDS.'
4. 'And how were you travelling?'
A. 'I was driving my Ford Sierra motor car.'
5. 'Where, on that road, were you at that time?'
A. 'I was approaching the junction of the main LEEDS road with the PANNAL road.'

Note how within five questions the officer has all but one of the factual details. Now he moves on to discover any offence detail, thus:

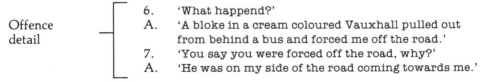

Offence detail

6. 'What happend?'
A. 'A bloke in a cream coloured Vauxhall pulled out from behind a bus and forced me off the road.'
7. 'You say you were forced off the road, why?'
A. 'He was on my side of the road coming towards me.'

The interviewing officer has now established prima facie evidence of an offence (careless driving).

2. Additional allegations (relevant facts in addition to points to prove)

When interviewing non-suspects *additional allegations* should never be overlooked as invariably there are matters, in addition to offence and factual detail which are important, particularly if there is to be a court appearance.

In assault cases for example, complainants will often allege that their attacker was drunk, had a violent temper, was jealous or was angered by some apparently innocuous incident. Similarly in theft cases, witnesses and complainants often tell of the Accused acting suspiciously prior to, during or after stealing. All these facts are important and should not be missed.

In addition, in many cases witnesses will often allege that the Accused made certain utterances which are always relevant and should not be overlooked. These points can be missed unless you ask the questions in much the same manner as the interviewing officer does in the road accident interview, thus:

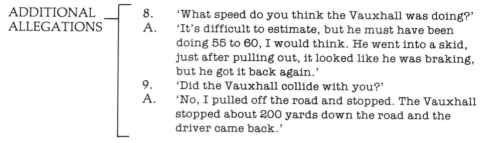

ADDITIONAL ALLEGATIONS

8. 'What speed do you think the Vauxhall was doing?'
A. 'It's difficult to estimate, but he must have been doing 55 to 60, I would think. He went into a skid, just after pulling out, it looked like he was braking, but he got it back again.'
9. 'Did the Vauxhall collide with you?'
A. 'No, I pulled off the road and stopped. The Vauxhall stopped about 200 yards down the road and the driver came back.'

The interviewing officer has gathered details of additional allegations (relevant facts in addition to points to prove) but in addition the witness has mentioned the offender and the interviewing officer immediately picks up this point making the interview naturally flow, thus:

Factual detail

10. 'What was he like?'
A. 'Young bloke, fair hair, sports jacket with a crest on the pocket.'
11. 'Would you recognise him again?'
A. 'I'll never forget him.'

ADDITIONAL ALLEGATIONS

12. 'Did he speak to you?'
A. 'Yes, he said it was his fault and that he had taken a chance. He said he was sorry.'

The first two questions round off factual detail and identify the driver of the offending Vauxhall, while the final question and answer provide yet more additional allegations to put to the offender. Bear in mind that when a written offence statement is taken from this particular witness the utterances alleged to have been made by the Accused will be recorded in 'direct speech' if at all possible.

By considering additional allegations the interviewing officer has naturally led himself on to the next objective to be covered in the interview.

3. Thinking it through

Here the interviewing officer is considering, as he always must, what other or further information might be of assistance to the decision maker. Relevant facts in addition to points to prove are again most important, some typical examples are as follows:

In theft and assault cases the relationship between the aggrieved and the alleged offender can often be most relevant. In motoring cases, the state of the road surface, the weather, the traffic conditions and even the driving experience, or lack of it, of the non-suspect, can all be relevant in assisting the decision maker.

Our interview continues, covering these very points.

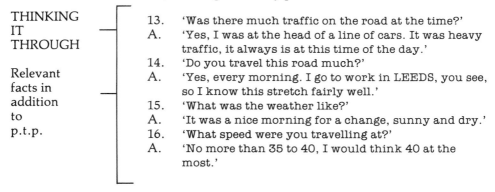

THINKING IT THROUGH

Relevant facts in addition to p.t.p.

13. 'Was there much traffic on the road at the time?'
A. 'Yes, I was at the head of a line of cars. It was heavy traffic, it always is at this time of the day.'
14. 'Do you travel this road much?'
A. 'Yes, every morning. I go to work in LEEDS, you see, so I know this stretch fairly well.'
15. 'What was the weather like?'
A. 'It was a nice morning for a change, sunny and dry.'
16. 'What speed were you travelling at?'
A. 'No more than 35 to 40, I would think 40 at the most.'

Because the Accused is not present means that at times the interviewing officer must be the 'devil's advocate', acting for the Accused and ensuring that the interview is being conducted fairly. *This is important*. The following point from the content of the interview should never be overlooked.

4. Defences

Defences must always be considered, both with suspects and non-suspects, for two reasons.

1. There sometimes are genuine reasons why people take a certain course of action which subsequently turns out to be against the law.
2. You should, at an early stage, try to establish whether or not it is alleged a defence exists as it is often only at such an early stage that the defence can be properly checked.

With the subject of defences you have to perform the delicate balancing act of searching for the truth on the one hand, but not suggesting that a particular defence exists on the other. This is easily achieved by giving the person questioned the opportunity to *raise a defence* when answering questions that do not directly contain that defence. (This method of questioning is covered in detail later in the chapter.)

Examples which illustrate this delicate search for defences with a non-suspect are as follows;

In assault cases the question 'Is there any reason why this man hit you?' is preferred to 'Did he hit you in self-defence?' or 'Did you provoke him?'

Similarly, in theft cases to ask the question 'Can you think of any good reason why he [the thief] took the property?' is preferred to 'Has he [the thief] a claim of right to this property?'

The main point that I am trying to make is that neither by inflection nor by content should you attempt to suggest a certain response and at all times you should be striving to be scrupulously fair. Let us see how the interviewing officer in the road accident interview tackles this point.

DEFENCES
17. 'Can you think of any reason why the Vauxhall pulled out in this manner?'
A. 'No, if he'd looked, he must have seen me.'
18. 'What about the fact that it was a sunny day, could that have had some bearing on it?'
A. 'Was he dazzled by the sun, do you mean, no I wouldn't think so. On this stretch the sun is to my right, so it wouldn't have been shining in his eyes. He certainly didn't mention that after the incident, anyway.'

5. One more question

It is good, professional, practice to work on the assumption that, at the end of the interview and before any written statement, *there is always one more question to be asked*.

By adopting this simple rule and in order to discover what that one more question is, you will naturally check items (1) to (4) of the *content of an interview* and ensure that all the necessary points, we have discussed so far, have been covered.

In addition, by using this one more question technique, you will find that it breeds in you a constructive questioning approach to your own performance which in turns leads to informed self-criticism and self-improvement.

The interviewing officer in the road accident case has considered his interview thus far and considers that his one more question is as follows:

ONE MORE QUESTION
19. 'Were you injured in the incident?'
A. 'No but my car was damaged.'

6. A statement in writing

Having completed the oral interview and obtained the story of the accident a written offence statement must now be completed and signed as without such a document, little can be achieved. However, there is another much more subtle reason for **a statement in writing**.

Although not wishing to deter the non-suspect from making a written statement, it is only right, early in the enquiry, to inform him or her of the effect of such a course of action, which is the possibility of a court appearance.

You will find that the overwhelming majority of non-suspects are only too anxious to make and sign a written statement and will not be deflected from such a course. If a non-suspect is less than keen to give a signed written statement it is as well to know it at the earliest stage and, further, this should make you look more closely at both the non-suspect and his complaint. Our interviewing officer covers this point in the following manner:

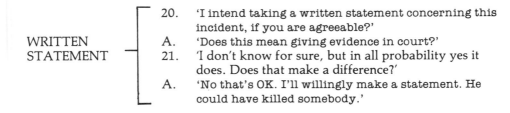

	20.	'I intend taking a written statement concerning this incident, if you are agreeable?'
WRITTEN STATEMENT	A.	'Does this mean giving evidence in court?'
	21.	'I don't know for sure, but in all probability yes it does. Does that make a difference?'
	A.	'No that's OK. I'll willingly make a statement. He could have killed somebody.'

That ends the interview of the non-suspect and although I accept that in most such interviews there are bound to be some scene-setting questions and utterances by the interviewing officer designed to put the interviewee at ease, the whole point of the method of interviewing I have outlined above is to focus your mind on the fact that questioning should be *relevant and pertinent not aimless and pointless*.

Quite obviously, a record is not kept of interviews with non-suspects, but I have recorded one to illustrate how the system works for non-suspect as well as suspect.

Second interview – the suspect

Let us together now look at how that same system of interviewing applies to the alleged offender in the same road accident case.

1. Method of approach

Having properly interviewed the non-suspect the interviewing officer is well aware that the suspect has possibly committed an offence of careless driving. Using the 'method of approach' and in answer to Question (4) *'How do I prove the offence?'* he arrives at the answer factual detail plus offence detail and asks his questions, thus:

METHOD OF APPROACH	1.	'Where were you on Monday, 31st March 19 – – , at about 8.30 a.m.?'
	A.	'I was travelling along the LEEDS to HARROGATE road, near PANNAL.'
	2.	'In which direction were you travelling?'
	A.	'Towards HARROGATE.'

The time, day, date and location have all been covered in these two simple questions (factual detail) and the next question will positively identify the offender as well as glean obvious offence detail.

Factual/Offence Detail	3.	'Were you driving a Vauxhall motor car, Regd No. KAD 113Y, along that road, at that time?'
	A.	'Yes I was.'

The officer has now identified, positively, the alleged offender and further has covered the following 'points to prove'.

1. The suspect (offender) was a 'driver'.
2. The suspect was driving a 'motor car'.
3. The suspect was driving 'on a road'.

All that important information has been gleaned from one simple question. The next question, now after caution, pin-points the exact location of the suspected offence, thus:

Factual Detail

4. CAUTION
'At that time, were you approaching the traffic lights which control the junction of the main LEEDS to HARROGATE road with the PANNAL ASH road?'
A. 'Yes I was.'

Now *all* the factual detail has been covered in the interview, plus much basic offence detail. In order to cover the remaining points to prove the officer asks as follows:

Offence Detail

5. 'It is alleged that you pulled out from behind a bus on the approach to the traffic lights, in the face of oncoming traffic. Did you do that?'
A. 'Yes, I took a chance.'

See how within five questions the interviewing officer has covered *all* the factual detail and all the basic offence detail required in this particular case. The interview now moves naturally on to cover the other relevant facts raised by the non-suspect of the vehicle possibly skidding, its speed and alleged admissions by the suspect under the next heading.

2. Additional allegations (relevant facts, etc)

ADDITIONAL ALLEGATIONS

6. 'It is alleged that at one stage you attempted to brake and your car began to skid. Is that right?'
A. 'Yes, that did happen.'
7. 'One of the witnesses alleges you were travelling quite fast, he thinks about 55 to 60 m.p.h., prior to this incident. What do you say?'
A. 'I was pushing on, yes, perhaps 50, not 55 though.'
8. 'After this incident you spoke to a car driver and he says, you said to him, "It was my fault, I took a chance". Did you say that?'
A. 'I said that I was in the wrong, yes.'

3. Thinking it through

By considering all the questions under this heading, but in particular the last question 'What information does he [the decision maker] need, to make that decision?' the interviewing officer should *anticipate* the needs of the decision maker. This naturally leads the officer to consider relevant facts in addition to points to prove, thus:

THINKING IT THROUGH
Relevant facts in addition to p.t.p.

9. 'You have said you were pushing on. Was there any reason for this?'
A. 'I was getting a bit late for an appointment.'
10. 'Do you remember what the weather conditions were, at the time?'
A. 'Yes it was dry and sunny.'

4. Defences

Here again the interviewing officer has to be most careful in trying to establish whether there is a defence and not suggesting that defence. Note how in the following the officer asks 'Is your car mechanically sound?' rather than 'Is the reason for your careless driving a mechanical failure?'

Similarly, the final question in this section is preferred to 'Did you have some temporary physical disbility which caused you to drive in this manner?'

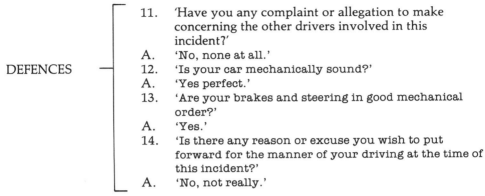

DEFENCES

11. 'Have you any complaint or allegation to make concerning the other drivers involved in this incident?'
A. 'No, none at all.'
12. 'Is your car mechanically sound?'
A. 'Yes perfect.'
13. 'Are your brakes and steering in good mechanical order?'
A. 'Yes.'
14. 'Is there any reason or excuse you wish to put forward for the manner of your driving at the time of this incident?'
A. 'No, not really.'

5. One more question

In order to ask this final question the interviewing officer has scanned what the non-suspect has said and has noticed a point he has not covered in the interview. This is now remedied.

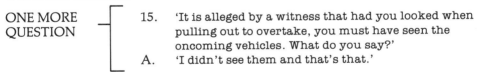

ONE MORE QUESTION

15. 'It is alleged by a witness that had you looked when pulling out to overtake, you must have seen the oncoming vehicles. What do you say?'
A. 'I didn't see them and that's that.'

6. A statement in writing

In all police interviews it is good practice to give the suspect the opportunity of making a written statement, although with the increased use of contemporaneous notes and tape recorders the practice of making written statements has diminished. However, if such a statement is made it will obviously need to be under caution and comply with the requirements of PACE. The interviewing officer in the road accident interview deals with this matter in the following manner:

STATEMENT IN WRITING

16. 'Do you wish to make a written statement?'
A. 'Yes, I think I do.'
17. 'Do you wish to write it yourself or would you prefer to dictate it?'
A. 'I'll dictate it to you.'

That concludes this section of the chapter, dealing with the content of the interview. It is interesting, yet again, to note how little is required in an interview, if it is carried out correctly; there were only 21 questions and answers in the first interview and 17 in the second.

The final part on the skill of interviewing deals with the manner in which you question and respond to answers, during the course of an interview.

Simple guidelines

Although this section is entitled **simple guidelines** the matters touched upon are extremely important. You will find that all the points outlined will be:

— of use to you throughout the rest of your service; and
— a firm base for further, more advanced training in police skills.

---

1.   One question at a time

You will find that although to ask an omnibus question is not strictly incorrect, answers to such questions are invariably not clear and, particularly when examined in court, are open to misinterpretation. When interviewing suspect and non-suspect alike, therefore, it is good technique to ask *short, to the point, uncomplicated* questions. The following is an example of how not to interview a suspect in an assault case.

> 'It is alleged you hit the complainant in the face, punched him in the stomach and then kicked him. This was a completely unprovoked attack. What have you got to say about it?'

This is so obviously wrong that the correct *one question at a time* needs little further comment from me in this example, thus:

1. 'It is alleged you hit him in the face, did you?'
2. 'It is alleged you punched him in the stomach, did you?'
3. 'It is alleged you kicked him, did you?'
4. 'It is alleged this was a totally unprovoked attack. What do you say?'

Similarly compare these two examples, taken from the interview of a suspect in a reckless case:

WRONG TYPE OF QUESTIONING
'The other driver says you were doing about 90 m.p.h., that your car was all over the road and at one point, you went into a four wheeled skid. Is that right?'

RIGHT TYPE OF QUESTIONING
1. 'It is alleged you were travelling at 90 m.p.h. What do you say?'
2. 'It is alleged your car was all over the road. What do you say?'
3. 'It is alleged that at one point, you went into a four wheeled skid. Did you?'

2. Do not suggest answers

In order to explain properly the significance of this point I would refer you again to '..*the object of a police interview is to establish the truth*'. Always remember, that is your prime responsibility.

I have already stated, but make no apology for repeating, that no question should be asked whether of a suspect or non-suspect, which, by content or inflection, suggests an answer. *This is an important point.* Examine the following two examples:

> WRONG   'Did the man who stole your bag have on a red flecked jacket?'
> RIGHT   'Describe what the man who stole your bag was wearing.'
> WRONG   'When the two youths pushed you to the ground you obviously began to scream?'
> RIGHT   'You've told me the two youths pushed you to the ground. What did you do at that time, if anything?'

The *wrong* question in both the above examples, invites the non-suspect to give an answer that has been suggested by the investigating officer. Believe me if you, as a police officer, suggest to a person that a certain answer is required, nine times out of ten you will get that answer. This is wrong, *never do it*.

The *right* method of questioning, in both the above examples, on the other hand, makes the potential witness think about the incident and further allows the investigating officer to test the strength and truth of the complaint.

A similar method of questioning should be adopted when interviewing a suspect, as the following two examples illustrate:

> WRONG   'You obviously used a screwdriver to open the window?'
> RIGHT   'How did you manage to open the window?'
> WRONG   'We have recovered the stolen video in the second-hand shop next to Barclays Bank.'
> RIGHT   'What did you do with the stolen video?'

By examining both of the above *wrong* questions, you should be able to see that the interviewing officer is throwing away an important evidential point in that *he is telling the suspect details of the offence.* Any answers he subsequently obtains will not confirm that it is the true offender in front of him; in fact, by suggesting answers, an innocent person could be made to appear to be the offender.

However, by asking the questions in the *right* manner, *evidence*, in the form of information, *known only to the offender*, might well be forthcoming and thus the truth will be established.

3. Dealing with the negative

There will be occasions, usually with suspects, when you find that you are being put off either by a stony silence, or the words 'no comment' being given as answers to the questions you are putting.

Regardless of such an attitude, as far as possible, *all* the points listed in *the content of an interview* should be covered and the suspect's response, or lack of it, noted, as in the following example:

QUESTION 'Were you the driver of an Austin Metro motor car, Regd No. A667 HOD, on Monday, 31st March 19 — —?'
ANSWER 'No comment.'
QUESTION 'At about 2.30 p.m. you were driving along the M5 just South of Birmingham. Is that right?'
ANSWER 'No comment.'

The method of dealing with non-suspects who refuse to describe what they have experienced has already been covered in 'negative statements' in Chapter 3.

4. The oblique method of questioning

This method of questioning has already been touched on, earlier in the chapter when dicussing defences. Often when trying to establish an important point, a safe and true method is to ask a series of seemingly bland questions, gradually tightening down to the particular point.

This method of questioning is often used by interviewing officers in cases where they believe they already know the answer to a particular question. However, in order to avoid suggesting an answer and to establish the truth they test, by using this **oblique method of questioning**.

The next example shows this technique being used where, in connection with the questioning of a witness concerning the identification of a man who has broken into her house, the interviewing officer is already aware that a suspect has been arrested in the area. The suspect is 21 years old.

QUESTION 'Can you describe the intruder?'
ANSWER 'Not very well, he was a young man.'
QUESTION 'What age?'
ANSWER 'I don't know, quite young.'
QUESTION 'How young, 20s, 30s, 40s?'
ANSWER 'Twenty to thirty I would say.'
QUESTION 'Early 20s or late 20s?'
ANSWER 'More early 20s.'
QUESTION 'Can you be more specific?'
ANSWER 'No that's the best I can do.'

Similarly the same system is used when questioning a suspect who has tricked his way into a house, by saying he was coming to inspect the gas meter:

QUESTION	'How did you get in?'
ANSWER	'She let me in.'
QUESTION	'Just like that?'
ANSWER	'She said come in.'
QUESTION	'I know she said come in, but why, you were a complete stranger?'
ANSWER	'I told her I was from the Electricity board.'
QUESTION	'Are you sure that's right?'
ANSWER	'Well the gas or the electricity.'
QUESTION	'Which was it?'
ANSWER	"Thinking about it now, it was the gas.'

The two examples above should show you how the interviewing officer is not trying to trick either the suspect or the non-suspect. He is, in fact, testing both the knowledge that he has and that of the person he is interviewing. In short he is trying to establish the truth.

---

5. Being flexible

I have already stated that prepared lists of questions and aide-mémoires are a help in police interviews. However, although as the interviewing officer, you will have a plan of your intended interview based on the *content of the interview*, always be flexible enough so as to be able to respond to and cope with any unexpected turn in the interview.

Such unplanned areas in an interview can be caused by the person who is being interviewed suddenly offering some unexpected piece of information, adopting an attitude not anticipated or discussing some totally unforeseen point.

Whatever the case, *flexibility* means:

1. Being prepared for this possibility.
2. Being able to cope with it (i.e. continue to conduct the interview correctly).
3. Being able to bring the interview back, on course, so that all the relevant points are covered.

6. Be dispassionate

It is sometimes very difficult when interviewing suspects and non-suspects alike, to be totally dispassionate. Nevertheless, as police officers you must always be so.

It is so easy to identify with non-suspects and compassion, genuinely felt, can quickly turn to sympathy, which in turn leads to a non-professional attitude being adopted.

Similarly, with persons suspected of particularly horrific or callous crimes, disgust and anger are emotions which are naturally felt, but which lead to a distorted approach and impede an officer in the correct execution of his duty.

However difficult it may be always *be dispassionate*.

You have now completed the teaching on *interviewing*, perhaps the most important of all police skills.

Never believe that you are incapable of properly interviewing anyone. If you plan and prepare your interviews in the manner described in this chapter they will become relevant, concise and accurate.

However long you serve as a police officer, you will continue to learn and improve your interviewing technique.

The system you have been shown in this chapter, linked as it is with the skills of statement writing and report construction, provides you with a reliable bedrock upon which to build. Trust the system, it will never let you down.

Improving your skills

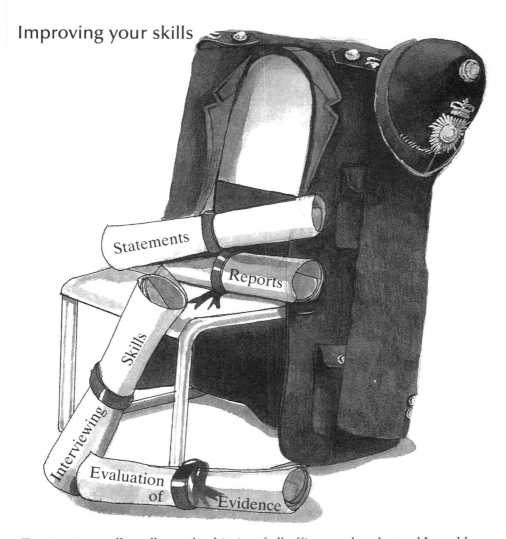

To interview really well must be the aim of all officers and to that end I would draw your attention to the points listed below which, I believe, can assist you.

1. *Contemporaneous notes LOCKE* (page 126) **15
   Recapitulation as to what has happened in the past is a good habit to adopt. It avoids any suggestion that the person to whom you are talking is not aware of the subject under discussion.

2. *Contemporaneous notes LOCKE* (page 128) **16
   Always make a note of everything of significance in an interview. This will include such things as periods of silence, conferences held by the defendant with his solicitor, breaks for coffee or tea and visits to the toilet. Instances of this kind occur in the contemporaneous notes of the other two reports.

3. *Contemporaneous notes MORRIS* (page 149) **17
   The phrase, 'Can you tell me in your own words what happened?' can be most potent to use. It invites either a suspect or non-suspect to *tell you* what happened. It is suprising what people will say if you give them such an invitation.

4. *Contemporaneous notes HURFORD* (page 178) **18
This is a deliberately poor question. It includes two parts (i.e. (1) Do you recall two men standing behind you? and (2) who later grabbed hold of you?). Questions should, if at all possible, be short and require only one answer. Keep it simple.

5. *Contemporaneous notes HURFORD* (page 180) **19
From this question onwards the interviewing officer is in full flight, covering important points and, equally important, inducing from the suspect the finer detail of the offence. The passage from point **19 to point **21 is particularly good.

6. *Contemporaneous notes HURFORD* (page 182) **20
This is a very good question, was probably unplanned, but the officer is flexible enough to respond to the previous answer with a most telling question. Apart from **18 mentioned above, this is a very good interview by the officer.

7. *In order to illustrate the need for the one more question* rule, I have deliberately left out of each of the interviews in the reports in Part 2 of this book, what I consider to be an important question. By using the methods outlined in this chapter you are invited to try to discover what those questions might be. If you are disinclined to attempt this exercise, the answers are printed below.

'Shoplifting' report

There are two significant points which you should consider. First, the offender LOCKE initially stated that she had forgotten to pay for the stolen pieces of steak and, for a while, it looked as though it would be difficult to prove 'dishonesty' on her part. However, the second point, if noticed, completely destroys this defence and it is the entry in the custody record showing that she had in her possession only 56 pence at the time of her arrest. The items she allegedly stole are worth £7.55. I would suggest that the 'one more question' to ask here would be concerning this lack of money (e.g. *'How did you intend to pay for this steak, you haven't enough money?'*).

'Accident' report

A very *relevant fact in addition to point to prove* in most accident cases, is the speed of a vehicle prior to or at the time of an accident. The interviewing officer, in this case, has skirted around this subject but has never asked the alleged offender at what speed he was travelling. The 'one more question' I consider in this case is concerned with the speed of the offending vehicle (e.g. *'What speed were you travelling at, prior to the accident?'*).

'Grievous bodily harm' report

Although the investigating officer has carried out a particularly good interview and covered almost all the required points for a successful prosecution, in my opinion, he has missed one very important question. The clue to what this question might be and its true significance is to be found in the entry on the collator's card, describing how the offender has used a bottle in a previous assault. All witnesses say that the offender took the bottle from his pocket. These two facts suggest that the alleged offender is in the habit of carrying and using such a weapon. It seems natural to ask *'Why were you carrying an empty beer bottle in your pocket?'* and that, I would suggest, is the 'one more question' in this particular report.

8 Evaluating evidence

The main object of this chapter is to provide you with a sure-fire method of evaluating the worth of a case, at any stage in an investigation. You should, as a professional police officer, be in a position to check properly the worth of your own work and this chapter shows you how to achieve that. The following points are discussed:

1. The three classifications of evidence in a case.
2. A method by which evidence is evaluated.
3. The three areas of evidence to be evaluated.

Within the first two years of your service you will not be required, formally, to evaluate the worth of the work you submit. Others will check and remark on its worth.

However, I am suggesting to you that you should, from the outset, cultivate in yourself the skill of *evaluating the worth* of a case. After all, you are now, after seven chapters of this book, in possession of virtually all the information any checker needs to evaluate a case, so why not do it yourself?

Further, there is no need to wait until the moment you submit a file or a report on an incident to carry out a check. You can and should evaluate your own performance, or the worth of a case, at many stages in an investigation. This can be done simply by applying the methods outlined in this chapter. By so doing you will automatically improve the quality of the work you produce.

Before you say that this is impossible you may be suprised to learn that if you have applied the teaching contained in the previous chapters, then you have already begun this *evaluation* process. The *one more question* rule, for example, from the *interviewing* chapter, shows this self-checking process at work.

This current chapter provides you, the operational officer, with a mental checklist applicable to *every* case that lies ahead of you. If you comply with it you will have rounded off your skill training and become a self-sufficient unit, working within the police organisation, but capable of individual competence.

Although it is the Crown Prosecution Service who now take the decision to prosecute or not, that should not mean that operational police officers ought not to evaluate the strengths and weaknesses of a particular enquiry upon which they are engaged.

In fact, I would say that it is imperative that such officers are in a position so to evaluate and, further, that it is vital that they do so. How else can they possibly decide on lines of enquiry and use of resources or discover shortcomings in the building of their case?

When deeply involved in an investigation it is not always easy to stand off and evaluate impartially the evidence you have to hand. However, I would urge you to attempt to do so, regardless of how damaging to your pride it may be. If you grasp the nettle and do so you will be continuing the thought process that began way back with the 'method of approach' and which now, with the 'evaluation of evidence', will see you successfully through to the conclusion of your investigation.

Classifying the evidence

When considering whether or not the evidence in a process report, a process report file or a DPP file supports the prosecution of an alleged offender, only three decisions can be arrived at:

1. *Sufficient — strong.*
2. *Sufficient — weak.*
3. *Insufficient.*

CLASSIFYING THE EVIDENCE

The worth of evidence can be classified in *only* three ways:

1. Sufficient   strong

2. Sufficient   weak

3. Insufficient

Because this chapter is concerned with evidence it follows that it only applies to the three types of report mentioned above.

Quite bluntly, there are only these three **classifications of evidence**, as set out above, and in order to illustrate all three and direct your thoughts along the correct lines, together, we shall look at a number of examples.

'Sufficient – strong'

Case (a)   'The football hooligan'

A football hooligan runs from a coach and attacks a man by using a broken bottle, causing serious injuries (deep cuts to the face and head). This is seen to happen by ten people, who are close to the incident. They are able to describe the assailant accurately and identify him to a nearby police officer, you, who arrests him, still in possession of the weapon. At the time of his arrest the offender says, after caution, *'I glassed him proper'*.

I think you would agree that this case, on the face of it, appears to come under the classification of **sufficient – strong** and indeed it is. The important question, however, is 'Why is it so classified?'

Later in this chapter we will look in more depth at classifications, but, briefly, the reasons supporting the fact that this case is a strong one are that in addition to the evidence of the complainant and his injuries, there is other good evidence, from the 10 witnesses plus your evidence, as the arresting officer, at the time of the arrest.

Confronted with such an incident you would no doubt consider yourself to be on *strong* ground and hopeful eventually of a conviction for 'wounding with intent' and I think you would be right.

However, let me inject a cautionary note here. No matter how strong a case may appear to be (and this is a strong case) *always consider possible weaknesses*. In this particular case it is possible that the offender *might* come up with a suggestion that he was 'provoked' or 'retaliated' or was acting in 'self-defence'.

In other words, as always, consider defences when collecting your evidence, even in such a strong case as this and, on a general note, always maintain an enquiring mind in relation to every incident, regardless of how strong it appears to be.

'Sufficient − weak'

Case (b)   'The stolen watch'

One man alleges that another has stolen his watch. The alleged offender states that, for whatever reason, he has a claim of right to the property. The loser denies that such a claim exists and demands prosecution of the offender and the return of the stolen property.

Case (c)   'The indecent assault'

A young boy (11 years) alleges that a man has indecently assaulted him. There is some medical evidence to support that the boy has been sexually assaulted although it does not incriminate, directly, the man. The boy identifies the suspect, who strongly denies the charge, although he admits to being in the area at the time of the assault.

After reading the synopsis of the two above cases, consider the phrase 'one man's word against another' as it certainly applies in both cases.

In both the theft and the indecent assault case, prima facie, there would appear to be *sufficient* evidence to support a case against each suspect. However, neither case can be said to be strong, in fact, as they stand, both are **sufficient − weak.**

In the 'stolen watch' case the suspect has produced the defence of 'claim of right' to the property. Who is to be believed, the loser or the suspect?

You, as the investigating officer, would certainly not let the matter rest there, I am sure. In practice the obvious course of action would be to investigate in greater depth both the allegation and the defence by further interviews, not only with the complainant and suspect but with other persons who might have pertinent knowledge. After all, **the object of any police interview is to establish the truth, be it supportive or otherwise of an allegation or complaint.**

The same procedure would need to be adopted with the indecency case which again is one person's word against another's. In this instance, despite being able to include the 'special evidence' of 'early complaint', the case is weak. You would no doubt consider the worth of further enquiries in the area of the assault, the possibility of witnesses being discovered and the likelihood of forensic evidence at the alleged scene.

In addition, though probably not admissible, background enquiries into both the complainant and the suspect, would be of help to the decison maker and possibly help in securing the truth.

The whole point is that you should recognise not only that a case is sufficient − weak but *why* it is so classified and *what* you need to do, *if possible*, to remedy the situation. Later in this chapter both these latter points will be discussed in depth.

'Insufficient'

Case (d)   'The burglar'

A burglary is known to have occurred and the suspect can be proved to have been in the area at the time for no good reason (in the middle of the night). The burglary is one of a series of five, three of which are admitted by the suspect. The only evidence against the suspect on this particular burglary is a finger print, which identifies the suspect, but with insufficient detail for proof in a court.

There will be occasions, throughout your service, when apparently blatant offenders will escape the due process of the law and you will feel frustrated and cheated.

The first thing I would advise is that you classify the evidence in the case and if, as in the above case, you come to the conclusion that there is **insufficient** evidence to support a prosecution, recognise that fact.

You are then faced with the problem of what else can be done and I would expect you to act positively and adopt the same attitude I advised when considering the 'sufficient — weak' cases. You would, I hope, consider any further or different lines of enquiry which might reveal evidence, ensure that your interviews of all persons had been exhaustive and check to see that all the evidence available had been gathered.

If at the end of this re-appraisal you still came to the conclusion that there was insufficient evidence then so be it. You would have done your best and that is all that is required of you.

Finally, be prepared for feelings of frustration and disappointment, these are natural reactions but do not allow them to flourish or affect your conduct.

An obsessive desire to prosecute a suspected offender, *by any means whatsoever, regardless of the truth,* is dangerous, unhealthy and wrong. Such conduct is contrary to all you have been taught and is definitely not required by the public you serve.

You have now learned of three classifications of evidence. As I stated before, you should not wait until the end of an enquiry before carrying out the classification process. By continually questioning yourself about the worth of a case, right from the very start and in particular by referring to the 'method of approach' and 'thinking it through', you will, constantly, be updating yourself on the strength of your enquiry and evaluating your own performance.

Evaluating the evidence

When evaluating the worth of the evidence in a process report, a process report file, or a DPP file, the following must be considered before a decision can be made:

1. The *main evidence*.
2. The *additional evidence*.
3. The *correct presentation* of the evidence.

In order to *classify* the evidence, in the manner I have just outlined, you need to be able to judge the value of it and in order to do that the evidence, in *any* of the cases you deal with, can be divided into three sections, which are set out above.

Little more need be said in this particular part of the chapter except that by dividing up the evidence in this manner you will be cultivating in yourself a clinical approach to case building, not based on emotion or personal interest and that should be your aim.

Let us look at the three sections into which the evidence has been placed for evaluation purposes.

1. The main evidence

This always consists of:

(a) The factual detail.
(b) The offence detail.

Evaluating the evidence

When evaluating evidence

consider:

1. The **main evidence**

2. The **additional evidence**

3. The **correct presentation**

You will know from as early as Chapter 2 in this book that the *minimum* requirement for any offence to be proved is that which is found within the jigsaw design, namely factual detail plus offence detail and that this minimum requirement is the foundation for *all* offences.

Therefore, when you examine a case, it is vital that you are able to see that all the required detail in these two sections is present, for, without just one piece of it, the whole case will fold.

By using the 'method of approach' at the scene of *all* incidents, you will obtain, if it exists, *at least*, the **main evidence**. If this is achieved it means that there is 'sufficient' evidence to prove a case.

In the 'careless driving case' in Part 2 of this book, for example (pages 136 — 155) it was necessary for the investigating officer to prove the existence of the main evidence, which, in this particular case comprised:

— The time, day, date and location of the alleged offence.
— The identity (Gordon MORRIS) of the alleged offender.
— That MORRIS was 'driving'.
— That he was driving a 'motor vehicle'.
— That he was driving 'on a road'.
— That he was driving 'without due care and attention'.

Often, as in this case, one statement will prove many, if not all of these points, but, whether it takes one or a hundred statements to prove them, *all* the required points of the main evidence must be present.

If you examine the statement of Christopher RELPH (pages 136 — 138) and the first six paragraphs of the statement of Police Constable ADAMS (page 146) you will see that all the above mentioned points have been covered.

The main evidence therefore establishes that there is sufficient evidence to prove a case.

2. The additional evidence

This can include any of the following:

(a) Relevant facts in addition to points to prove.
(b) Hearsay.
(c) Supporting evidence.
(d) Defences.
(e) Opinion.

In the same manner that the main evidence established whether or not there was sufficient evidence for a possible prosecution, so the additional evidence is used to establish whether the case is strong or weak. The headings listed (a) to (e) above are not new to you and I do not intend to go through each in detail. Chapters 3, 4, 5 and 7 illustrated in some depth how these self-same headings were used in statement construction, in report writing and in the skill of interviewing.

The presence, or lack, of any of these additional evidential points will affect the strength of a case. You are now aware that such evidence exists and, in the initial stages of an investigation, should secure it, if it is there to be found.

Further, throughout the course of the investigation, as well as at the end, you should continually be monitoring this 'strengthening' evidence so that by the time your investigation is complete, all that needs to have been done, will have been done.

Just a brief word, then, about each area of the additional evidence.

(a) Relevant facts in addition to points to prove

You may recall there were seven additional **relevant facts** which were grafted on to the jigsaw design. All are important and should be looked for in most process reports or process report files.

I would particularly draw your attention again to the fact *'Why something happened'* as it will encourage you to look for the 'reason behind the incident' which, in turn, should trigger in your mind, all of the other relevant facts.

(b) Hearsay

You have been told of the occasions when **hearsay** is formally allowed in offence statements and you should remember them.

The importance of the inclusion of other hearsay, although probably ultimately inadmissible in a court, has also been explained to you and I would repeat that such hearsay must be *relevant* to the case. Such inclusions can be of great assistance to a decision maker.

Ensure therefore, that irrelevant hearsay does not appear in your offence statements as its inclusion tends to exasperate and confuse. Relevant hearsay, whether or not it is later edited, can be most telling. Be disciplined and correct in your use of hearsay.

(c) Supporting evidence

This is probably the most important factor when assessing the strength of a case. You are already aware of the fact that '**the evidence of two or more persons is stronger than the evidence of one**' and that it is the manner of collecting such evidence which makes it so strong.

In all three of the reports in Part 2 of the book you will find examples of strong **supporting evidence**. When you come to examine this evidence bear in mind the fact that it was taken from each witness independently and with no prompting, in other words correctly. Similarly, when you are examining evidence in your own real-life cases, ensure that similar care has been taken. If it has not and there has been a danger of collusion or, through no one's fault, witnesses have got together and discussed the case before making statements, then draw the attention of the decision maker to this fact, in your report. After all, you are only being truthful.

However, in addition to supporting evidence supplied by witnesses, you will find in your investigations, other forms of evidence which support and strengthen a case, as follows:

— Forensic evidence (e.g. finger prints, fibres, DNA profiles, mechanical fit of objects and clothing and a host of other marks or signs at the scene of a crime) can assist, sometimes conclusively, in supporting the main evidence. Always be aware of the possibility of the existence of such evidence and never be afraid to seek advice or assistance in the search for it.

- Admissions by the Accused can be very strong supporting evidence and they need not necessarily be admissions as to the commission of an offence, but can include admissions which confirm details given by witnesses (e.g. Accused's actions or conduct prior to or after the commission of an offence, utterances made by the Accused, clothing worn, articles carried by or persons accompanying the Accused). Admissions of guilt by the Accused are obviously pieces of strong supporting evidence. Ensure that such admissions are obtained and recorded properly.
- Denials and lies told by the Accused can similarly be damning and evidence which shows that the Accused has not been truthful, in a material particular, again strongly supports the prosecution. Such denials and lies must be properly obtained and recorded if they are to be admissible.
- Hearsay evidence, in certain sexual cases, can be most supportive of a complaint. 'Early complaints' are accepted by courts as they tend to show the natural reaction of persons who have been sexually abused. The lack of such evidence will tend to weaken a case and should also prompt in you, the investigating officer, a cautionary, though not disbelieving, attitude to the complainant.

(d) Defences

It may seem odd to include defences in an evaluation of the strength of the evidence but if you, as the investigating officer, are concerned with the pursuit of the truth, then defences are of prime importance. Quite obviously if there is a defence to a particular offence then it should be covered in any report which you submit. Failure to do so will mean that the decision maker will probably return the file to you for this most important of points to be covered.

In the specimen reports at the rear of the book there are many examples where, within offence statements, defences have been considered and properly taken into account. Chapter 3, on statements, illustrated this point well, but the following are common examples, which may assist you in everyday incidents:

Theft cases. The usual defence is that the offender states that he has some claim of right to the stolen property. This can be partially negated by including in the offence statement of the loser phrase, '...no one had permission to take the [stolen item]...'.

Assault. A common defence to an assault charge is one of self-defence. This can be covered by including in the aggrieved's statement the phrase, '...there was no possible reason for this attack upon me, I had done nothing to provoke it...'.

Sexual assault. The usual defence is that the assaulted person gave consent to the act. Such a defence can be taken into account by including in statements the manner in which the aggrieved behaved at the time of the assault, thus, '...I screamed and tried to stop him...' or, '...I told him no but he just kept on...'. It is as well to add, however, if it is true, the following to such statements, '...I did not consent to [the act] neither did I give the impression that I consented or wanted to consent...'.

As I have already pointed out in Chapter 7, Interviewing skills, the subject of defences is a delicate one and the manner in which you deal with them has been fully covered in that chapter. Two further points are worth mentioning which do affect the strength of a case.

If an aggrieved person is unable to provide evidence which negates a defence then not only might that weaken a case, but it should place in your mind a question as to the veracity of that complaint.

Finally, although it may seem obvious, defences can, quite rightly, destroy the strongest of cases. It is as well to consider defences right at the outset of an enquiry.

(e) Opinion

Apart from the evidence given by experts, which is often of prime importance, evidence of **opinion** is the least weighty strengthener that you should consider.

Most opinion will be edited from your reports before a case arrives at court and it is in that light that you should consider the worth of it. Nevertheless, it should be included in the circumstances I have described in Chapter 3 as, again, it is of use to the decision maker.

The main evidence and the additional evidence are the two areas which will decide for you the worth and strength of your cases. It could be that you will arrive at this stage of evaluation with a very strong prosecution case only to find that much good work has been in vain, because you have failed at the final hurdle, namely:

---

3. The correct presentation

This will apply to:
(a)   Exhibits.
(b)   Cautions.
(c)   Interviews.

(a) Exhibits

You are well aware now of the correct, simple procedure for referring to exhibits in statements. Unless this is strictly adhered to, evidence, vital to your case, can be in jeopardy. With this easiest of procedures, this should never happen.

When checking your statements and reports, therefore, ensure that exhibits have been referred to and itemised correctly. If you don't, someone else will, usually the defence lawyer.

(b) Cautions

The Police and Criminal Evidence Act 1984 and the Codes of Practice stemming from it are unyielding in laying down exactly what is required of a police officer in the course of any investigation. There is no excuse for non-compliance and again much good work can be lost by a neglectful attitude.

You should not need to be told that the cautioning of a suspect at the correct time is of prime importance, both to the suspect and to you. After all if it is not done properly *at the time* it certainly cannot be corrected *afterwards*.

(c) Interviews

When evaluating the worth of your case, at whatever stage in your investigation, always consider the manner in which interviews have been carried out as well as their true worth.

The previous two paragraphs on cautions must obviously be considered and then run through, in your mind, the *content of the interview* and check to see if all the relevant points, as previously taught in the chapter on interviews, have been covered.

The *evaluating* process is now complete.

You are now in a position to look at a report or file and, working within the system you have been taught, give a considered opinion as to the worth of that case.

Don't, however, think that the evaluation of evidence is a process confined to a desk, at the end of an investigation.

You should, from the very first instant, be continually classifying and evaluating the worth and strength of any case upon which you are engaged, from the very simplest of offences to the most involved. By so doing:

— *You* will anticipate likely problems.
— *You* will remedy possible shortcomings.
— *You* will comply with required practices.

In fact you will suddenly discover that *you are in control and that is what the public expect from you.*

Improving your skills

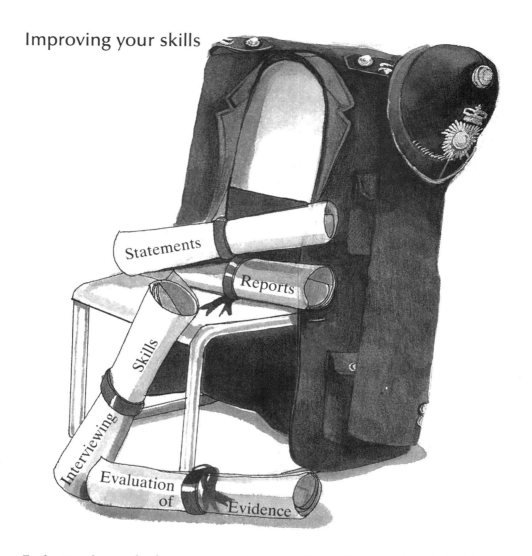

Evaluating the worth of a case, as you have seen, is merely a question of checking whether the more important areas of the four police skills are present in that case.

To that end I have set out a 'case planner', on page 106, based on this process, which evaluates the 'careless driving' case, set out in Part 2 of this book.

The design of this form is flexible in that under the section listing the various statements referred to, you may either tick the box or write in a page number.

Further, in relation to the section covering the offence detail, depending on the offence, the number of 'points to prove' may be more or less than the five I have listed in the example.

By continually referring to this form you, as the officer in this case, will know exactly:

1. The strengths or weaknesses of your case, which you can then highlight in a subsequent report.
2. Those areas of the enquiry still requiring further investigation.
3. The importance of particular witnesses.
4. That the correct procedures have been followed.

I would commend this form to you as its basic design can be applied to any of the cases with which you will deal.

Why not use it in your next case? Keep it with the statements and other documents and see if it helps you. I think you will find that it not only serves as a reliable checklist but also as a continual reminder of the whole police skill teaching.

The interesting point I discovered after completing the 'case planner' was that *only* Police Constable ADAMS had dealt with the question of defences. I should add that it is often difficult for a civilian witness to cover defences in such a case. Having said that, I think you will agree that this case is certainly **sufficient** — **strong**.

THE CASE PLANNER

STATEMENT OF:

	RELPH	UPTON	BOUNDY	HINDLE	ADAMS		
THE MAIN EVIDENCE							
Factual detail							
Time	*	*	*		*		
Day	*	*	*	*	*		
Date	*	*	*	*	*		
Place	*	*	*		*		
I/D of offender	*	*	*		*		
Offence detail							
1. Driving	*	*	*		**		
2. Motor vehicle	*	*	*		*		
3. On a road	*	*	*		*		
4. W/O due care	*	*	*		*****		
5.							
THE ADDITIONAL EVIDENCE							
Relevant facts	*****	*******	*****	**			
Hearsay	*	*	*	*			
Supporting evidence		*	*				
Defences					**		
Opinion	**	****	**				
THE CORRECT PRESENTATION							
Exhibits					GGA/1-3		
Cautions					**		
Interviews					*		

106

9 Conclusion

You have now completed all the teaching contained within this book on the four basic police skills.

It is impossible, I would suggest, to lay before you every type of incident with which you will be confronted and then give you the individual solution to each. This book has not even attempted that.

What it has set out to do is to provide you with a system of working and thinking that will atuomatically lead you to the correct solution for every incident you encounter.

For most of you reading this book, many years of service stretch ahead and, within those years, lie experiences, good and bad. Such is the way of police work.

Your period of service will encompass changes in legislation and procedures, improvements in technological and forensic aids and an ever-developing use of transport and communications. There will, no doubt, be shifts in the style of training and differing methods in the use of resources will be attempted.

If the last decade is anything to go by, ahead lie crises to which the service will have to respond and about which politicians, pressure groups, the media and the public itself will have views as varied as the political spectrum of this country.

Experts, many of whom have yet to don the blue uniform, will advise, suggest, cajole and bully the service, which will twist and turn as it seeks to conform and comply with the seemingly unending demands of our society.

Within the eye of this whirlwind of change stands the Constable, for whatever the colour of government, whatever the current fashion, whatever the new gadgetry the two responsibilities of the operational police officer remain the same.

The teaching within this book provides you, the operational police officers of today and tomorrow, with a codified method of working and thinking, enabling you to produce work to the very highest standard.

Whether we like it or not, that is the least the public have come to expect from us and that is what we should always be striving to achieve.

Part 2

Operational police skills: examples and specimens

<u>NEGATIVE POCKET NOTEBOOK ENTRY</u>

There has been a road traffic accident. The driver of
the offending vehicle, a Simca motor car, Regd No. A355 JHD
is Mr Christopher HOWARD. In the front passenger seat
of that vehicle is Phillip PERRY, who is most reluctant
to say anything about the accident. The following is the
pocket notebook entry of the investigating officer.

Sunday, 11th May 19--

11.40 a.m. High Road East, PRESTON, at the junction
            of Swallow Drive. Road accident.
            Interview of Phillip PERRY (b.18.8.58)
            electrician of 118 Northern Estate, PRESTON.

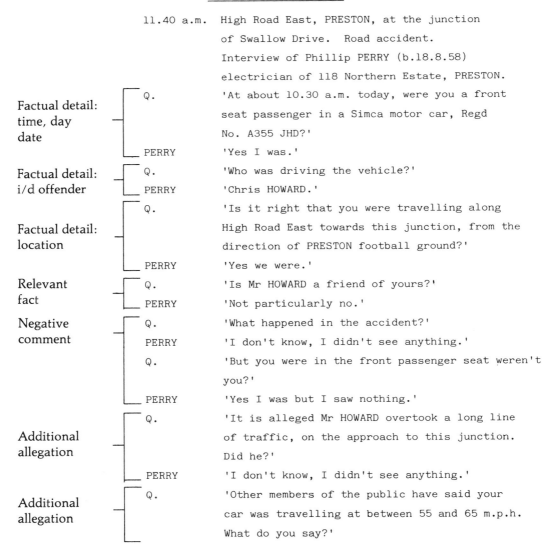

Factual detail: time, day date	Q. 'At about 10.30 a.m. today, were you a front seat passenger in a Simca motor car, Regd No. A355 JHD?'
	PERRY 'Yes I was.'
Factual detail: i/d offender	Q. 'Who was driving the vehicle?'
	PERRY 'Chris HOWARD.'
Factual detail: location	Q. 'Is it right that you were travelling along High Road East towards this junction, from the direction of PRESTON football ground?'
	PERRY 'Yes we were.'
Relevant fact	Q. 'Is Mr HOWARD a friend of yours?'
	PERRY 'Not particularly no.'
Negative comment	Q. 'What happened in the accident?'
	PERRY 'I don't know, I didn't see anything.'
	Q. 'But you were in the front passenger seat weren't you?'
	PERRY 'Yes I was but I saw nothing.'
Additional allegation	Q. 'It is alleged Mr HOWARD overtook a long line of traffic, on the approach to this junction. Did he?'
	PERRY 'I don't know, I didn't see anything.'
Additional allegation	Q. 'Other members of the public have said your car was travelling at between 55 and 65 m.p.h. What do you say?'

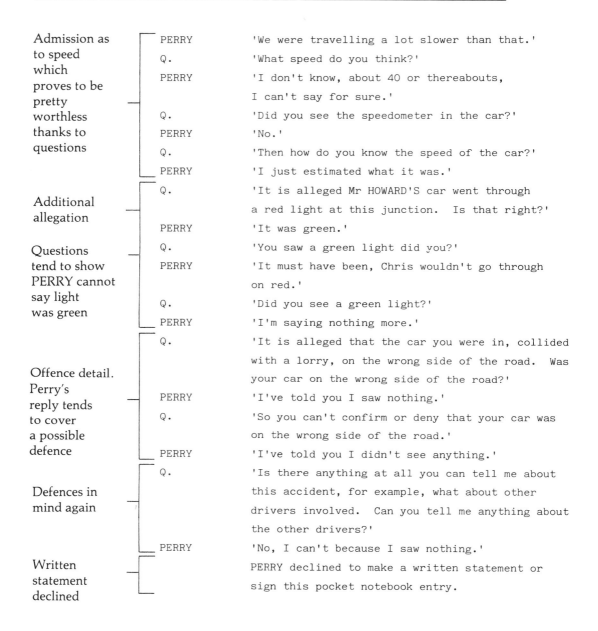

Admission as to speed which proves to be pretty worthless thanks to questions	PERRY	'We were travelling a lot slower than that.'
	Q.	'What speed do you think?'
	PERRY	'I don't know, about 40 or thereabouts, I can't say for sure.'
	Q.	'Did you see the speedometer in the car?'
	PERRY	'No.'
	Q.	'Then how do you know the speed of the car?'
	PERRY	'I just estimated what it was.'
Additional allegation	Q.	'It is alleged Mr HOWARD'S car went through a red light at this junction. Is that right?'
	PERRY	'It was green.'
Questions tend to show PERRY cannot say light was green	Q.	'You saw a green light did you?'
	PERRY	'It must have been, Chris wouldn't go through on red.'
	Q.	'Did you see a green light?'
	PERRY	'I'm saying nothing more.'
Offence detail. Perry's reply tends to cover a possible defence	Q.	'It is alleged that the car you were in, collided with a lorry, on the wrong side of the road. Was your car on the wrong side of the road?'
	PERRY	'I've told you I saw nothing.'
	Q.	'So you can't confirm or deny that your car was on the wrong side of the road.'
	PERRY	'I've told you I didn't see anything.'
Defences in mind again	Q.	'Is there anything at all you can tell me about this accident, for example, what about other drivers involved. Can you tell me anything about the other drivers?'
	PERRY	'No, I can't because I saw nothing.'
Written statement declined		PERRY declined to make a written statement or sign this pocket notebook entry.

Report A: Shoplifting

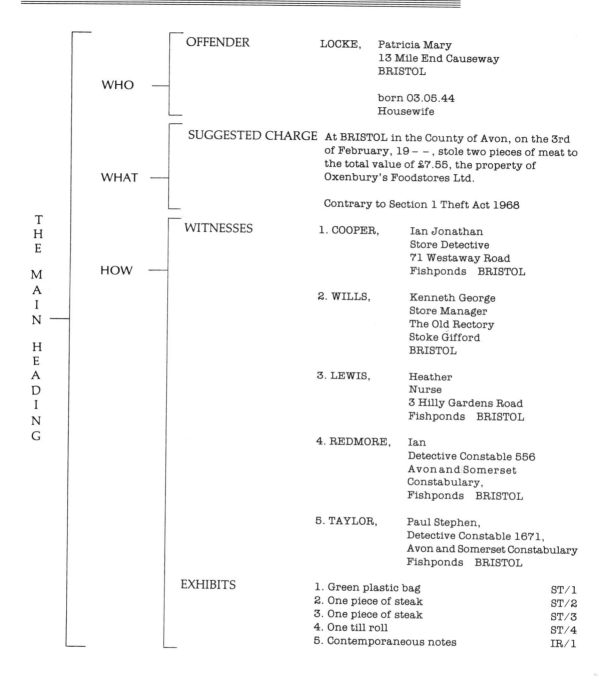

THE MAIN HEADING

WHO — OFFENDER
LOCKE,   Patricia Mary
13 Mile End Causeway
BRISTOL

born 03.05.44
Housewife

WHAT — SUGGESTED CHARGE
At BRISTOL in the County of Avon, on the 3rd of February, 19 – –, stole two pieces of meat to the total value of £7.55, the property of Oxenbury's Foodstores Ltd.

Contrary to Section 1 Theft Act 1968

HOW — WITNESSES
1. COOPER,   Ian Jonathan
Store Detective
71 Westaway Road
Fishponds   BRISTOL

2. WILLS,   Kenneth George
Store Manager
The Old Rectory
Stoke Gifford
BRISTOL

3. LEWIS,   Heather
Nurse
3 Hilly Gardens Road
Fishponds   BRISTOL

4. REDMORE,   Ian
Detective Constable 556
Avon and Somerset Constabulary,
Fishponds   BRISTOL

5. TAYLOR,   Paul Stephen,
Detective Constable 1671,
Avon and Somerset Constabulary
Fishponds   BRISTOL

EXHIBITS
1. Green plastic bag   ST/1
2. One piece of steak   ST/2
3. One piece of steak   ST/3
4. One till roll   ST/4
5. Contemporaneous notes   IR/1

THE SUMMARY

OTHER MATTERS

Label	Text

Brief introduction

Sir,
    This report concerns the alleged theft, by the above named LOCKE, of two pieces of meat, total value £7.55, from Oxenbury's Food Store at FISHPONDS on 3rd February 19 – – . Briefly the facts are as follows:

Factual detail

Offence detail: appropriates property

Accused's conduct
Supportive offence detail (dishonestly)

    At about 10.45 a.m. that day, the Accused was seen to enter the store by the store detective, the witness COOPER. He kept her under observation throughout the whole of the time she was in the store and saw her select a number of items from the display shelves, including the two pieces of steak. When LOCKE came to the check-out, COOPER noted that she failed to produce or pay for the two pieces of steak, he had earlier seen her select.
    Outside the store, he challenged LOCKE, who denied the theft, but agreed to accompany COOPER to the manager's office.
    The witness LEWIS was in the store at the time and actually saw the Accused place the stolen items into a plastic carrier bag (ST/1), instead of the wire basket, provided by the store.

Supportive offence detail/ exhibits

    The reporting officer attended and in the store manager's office, in the presence of the Accused, searched the plastic bag and found the two pieces of steak (ST/2 and 3), together with a till roll (ST/4), which clearly showed she had not paid for the meat.

Supportive offence detail (belonging to another)

    The manager of the store, the witness WILLS, supports the evidence of the brief interview of the Accused and the search which took place in his office, as does the witness COOPER. Further, WILLS gives evidence as to ownership and value of the stolen items.

Offence detail/ exhibit (permanently deprive)

    The Accused was arrested and taken to the Fishponds Police Station, where later, when interviewed, she made a full admission, details of which appear in the contemporaneous note of the interviewer (IR/1), taken by Detective Constable REDMORE.

Relevant facts for decision maker

    The Accused has one previous conviction recorded against her, details of which are attached. The store detective, Mr COOPER, has informed the police that he has long suspected this woman of stealing from this particular store.
    At the time of her arrest, the Accused had only 56 pence in her possession.

Current position of accused

    The Accused has not been charged, but has been bailed to re-appear at Fishponds Police Station, at 10.30 a.m. on Monday 24th February 19 – – .

Detective Constable 1671

STATEMENT FORM

Name .... Ian Jonathan COOPER ....

Address .... 71 Westaway Road, Fishponds, BRISTOL ....

Occupation .... Store detective ....   Age 44 yrs (b.27.8.41)

This statement (consisting of   3   pages each signed by me) is true to the best of my knowledge and belief and I make it knowing that if it is tendered in evidence I shall be liable to prosecution if I have wilfully stated in it anything which I know to be false or do not believe to be true.

Dated the ..... 3rd ... day of February .... 19.--.   ....

Signed ... I.J. COOPER ....

Relevant facts	I am employed as a store detective by Oxenbury's Food Store, my area of responsibility being mainly in the BRISTOL area.
Factual detail	On Monday, 3rd February 19-- I was on duty in the Fishponds branch which is a large self-service store.
Factual detail — i/d offender	At about 10.45 a.m. that morning, I saw a woman in a dark red overcoat enter the store. She was carrying a green plastic bag and a large leather handbag.
Relevant fact	As she entered the store I saw her pick up one of our wire baskets, in which shoppers are supposed to place articles they have selected to buy.
Relevant facts 'conduct of Accused'	I kept this woman under observation, from the time she entered the store, until she left, a period of about five or six minutes. During that time I saw that she selected the following items from the shelves in the store. I saw that she first selected three bars of chocolate, then walked around to the general foodstuffs department and selected one bag of sugar, one bag of flour, a box of salt and a packet of raisins. All these items she placed quite openly into the wire basket.
Offence detail (appropriates property)	The woman then walked to the meat counter and took from the display, two pieces of steak, which were contained in cellophane wrapped cardboard dishes. I saw her holding these two items in her right hand. At the

Signed ... I.J. COOPER ....

Offence detail (appropriates property)

same time she was holding the wire basket, her handbag and the plastic bag in her left hand.

Still holding the pieces of meat, in the manner I have described, the woman then walked towards the drinks display. I lost sight of her for about two to three seconds as she went around the end of the display shelf and, when I next saw her, I could see that the two pieces of meat were no longer in her hand. I further noticed that the green plastic bag was now in her right hand.

Offence detail 'appropriates property'

The woman stood looking at the display of drinks for about a minute and then went to the check-out. I followed her and stood about two feet away, as she checked out her purchases. I was able easily to see that she paid for all the items I have mentioned earlier, but did not pay for the two pieces of meat, which I was able to see were not in the wire basket, nor produced, by the woman, to the check-out girl.

Relevant fact 'conduct of the Accused' after commission of offence

I followed the woman, as she left the store and, immediately outside the main entrance I stopped her.

I said, 'I am a store detective. I have just been watching you in this store' (indicating Oxenbury's). 'I have seen you take two pieces of steak from a display in the store. You failed to pay for these two pieces of meat before leaving the store.'

The woman said, 'You're making a big mistake'.

I said, 'I would like you to accompany me to the manager's office so that this matter can be sorted out properly'.

The woman said, 'Yes, I'll come, but I've done nothing wrong'.

I then took the woman back with me to the manager's office.

Relevant admissible hearsay

In the presence and hearing of the woman, I   **1
said to the manager, Mr WILLS, 'This woman has just left the store without paying for two pieces of steak. I believe she has hidden the meat, somewhere on her person'.

Signed .... I.J. COOPER ....

Relevant
fact
conduct of
Accused

> The woman said, 'You're wrong, you're not searching me.'

Relevant
admissible
hearsay

> At 11.05 a.m. that same day Constable TAYLOR arrived in the office and I said, to the officer, in the presence and hearing of the woman, 'Earlier on today I kept this woman under observation, from the moment she entered this store, to the moment she left. During that time I saw her take from the display shelves, two pieces of steak. She did not place these items in the wire basket nor produce them for payment when she went to the check-out. She denies having the meat and has refused to allow me to search her.'

Supportive
evidence
(TAYLOR)

> Constable TAYLOR said, 'You have heard what this man says, what do you say?'
>
> He cautioned the woman, and she said, 'I haven't stolen anything'.
>
> Constable TAYLOR said, 'What is your name?'
>
> The woman said, 'PATRICIA LOCKE'.
>
> Constable TAYLOR said, 'Mrs LOCKE, can I look in your bag?'
>
> The woman said, 'If you must'.

Exhibits

> I then saw Constable TAYLOR take from the green plastic bag (ST/1) all the items I have previously described as well as two pieces of steak (ST/2 and 3), I had earlier seen the woman remove from the display shelf.
>
> In addition I saw Constable TAYLOR take a till receipt (ST/4) from the bag. At that time the woman said,

Relevant
fact
'conduct
of
Accused'

> 'Okay, so I've got the damn steak, so what'.
>
> Constable TAYLOR said, 'I am arresting you on suspicion of stealing these two pieces of steak'.
>
> He again cautioned the woman and she said, 'Okay'.
>
> Constable TAYLOR then left the store with the woman.

Irrelevant

> Later that day I went down to the station and made a statement about this matter.

Signed .... I.J. COOPER ....

STATEMENT FORM

Name .... Kenneth George WILLS ....

Address .... The Old Rectory, Stoke Gifford, BRISTOL ....

Occupation. Store manager ....   Age .50. yrs .(b.16.11.35)

This statement (consisting of 2 pages each signed by me) is true to the best of my knowledge and belief and I make it knowing that if it is tendered in evidence I shall be liable to prosecution if I have wilfully stated in it anything which I know to be false or do not believe to be true.

Dated the....3rd....day of..February.......................... 19.--...   ....

Signed........... K.G. WILLS ....

Relevant fact

        I am the store manager of Oxenbury's Food Store, at 44 Brunel Avenue, Fishponds, BRISTOL

Factual detail i/d of offender

        At about 11.00 a.m. on Monday, 3rd February 19-- I was in my office in the store, when Mr COOPER, our store detective, came to the office with a woman.
        The woman was wearing a dark red overcoat and I saw that she was carrying a green plastic bag. I think she had a handbag as well, but I cannot be sure. The woman was in her forties, slim with blondish hair. I would definitely recognise her again.   **2

Supportive evidence (COOPER)

        In the presence and hearing of the woman, Mr COOPER said, 'This woman has just left the store without paying for two pieces of steak. I believe she has hidden the meat, somewhere on her person.'
        The woman said, 'You're wrong, you're not searching me'.

Supportive evidence (TAYLOR)

        At 11.05 a.m. that same day Constable TAYLOR arrived in the office and Mr COOPER said, to him in the presence and hearing of the woman, 'Earlier on today I kept this woman under observation, from the moment she entered this store, to the moment she left. During that time I saw her take from the display shelves, two pieces of steak. She did not place these items in the wire basket nor produce them for payment when she went to the check-out. She denies having the meat and has refused to allow me to search her.'

Signed........... K.G. WILLS ....

119

Supportive evidence (TAYLOR)

> Constable TAYLOR said, 'You have heard what this man says, what do you say?'
>
> He cautioned the woman and she said, 'I haven't stolen anything'.
>
> Constable TAYLOR said, 'What is your name?'
>
> The woman said, 'PATRICIA LOCKE'.
>
> Constable TAYLOR said, 'Mrs LOCKE, can I look in your bag?'
>
> The woman said, 'If you must'.

Exhibits

> I then saw Constable TAYLOR take from the green plastic bag (ST/1) a number of items. Included in those items were two pieces of steak (ST/2 and 3).
>
> These two pieces of meat (ST/2 and 3) were in cardboard dishes, wrapped in cellophane, similar to the manner in which we wrap and display meat in this store.
>
> In addition to this I saw Constable TAYLOR take from the green plastic bag a till receipt (ST/4). At that

Supportive evidence (TAYLOR)

> time the woman said, 'Okay, so I've got the damn steak, so what'.
>
> Constable TAYLOR said, 'I am arresting you on suspicion of stealing these two pieces of steak'.
>
> He again cautioned the woman and she said, 'Okay'.
>
> Constable TAYLOR then left the store with the woman.

Offence detail 'property belonging to another'

Defences

> The value of the two pieces of meat is as follows. One piece (ST/2) is priced at £2.75, while the other piece (ST/3) is priced at £4.80. I noticed that Oxenbury's price tags were on the two pieces of meat, quoting these same prices.
>
> I can definitely say that both pieces of meat are the property of Oxenbury's Food Stores Ltd, and no one has permission to take these items, from the store, without paying for them.

Signed .... K.G. WILLS ....

STATEMENT FORM

Name .... Heather LEWIS

Address .... 3 Hilly Gardens Road, Fishponds, BRISTOL

Occupation........ Nurse   Age. 35 yrs (b.25.3.51)

This statement (consisting of 2 pages each signed by me) is true to the best of my knowledge and belief and I make it knowing that if it is tendered in evidence I shall be liable to prosecution if I have wilfully stated in it anything which I know to be false or do not believe to be true.

Dated the.....3rd...day of......... February .... 19.--.   ....

Signed........ H. LEWIS

Factual detail	At about 10.50 a.m. on Monday, 3rd February 19--, I was shopping in Oxenbury's Food Store, 44 Brunel Avenue, Fishponds, BRISTOL.
Irrelevant	I had to purchase some items for the old folk who live in the rest home for the elderly, where I work. Most of them are unable to get to the shops any more.
Factual detail i/d offender	While in the store I noticed a woman in a dark red overcoat. She was carrying a green plastic carrying bag, it was a dark colour anyway. She was also carrying a wire basket.
Relevant fact 'conduct of Accused'	What drew my attention to this woman was the fact that she had items of shopping in her wire basket, but she was also carrying, in her hand, two large pieces of steak.
Offence detail 'appropriation'	At this time I was at the end of the display shelves, where the meats are on display and close to the wines and spirits display. As this woman passed me, going towards the drinks section, I saw her put the two pieces of steak into the green plastic carrying bag.
Supportive exhibits	I have today been shown by Constable TAYLOR a green plastic carrying bag (ST/1) and can say that it appears identical to the one I saw being carried by the woman.
Supportive exhibits	Further I have been shown two pieces of steak (ST/2 and 3) and can say that they appear identical to the two I saw the woman place in the plastic bag.

**3

Signed.........H. LEWIS...............................

121

Factual
detail
i/d
offender

> I would describe the woman as being in her late thirties or early forties. She was about 5'9", slim build, light-coloured hair, cut short. She was wearing a red-coloured top coat. I think I would recognise her again.

Signed .... H. LEWIS ....

STATEMENT FORM

Name .... Stephen Paul TAYLOR ....

Address .... Avon and Somerset Constabulary, Fishponds, BRISTOL ....

Occupation ... Detective Constable 1671 .....   Age ..... Over 21 years ..

This statement (consisting of 2 pages each signed by me) is true to the best of my knowledge and belief and I make it knowing that if it is tendered in evidence I shall be liable to prosecution if I have wilfully stated in it anything which I know to be false or do not believe to be true.

Dated the .... 3rd .... day of ...... February .... 19.--.   ....

Signed ...... S.P. TAYLOR   D.C. 1671 ......

Factual detail	At 11.05 a.m. on Monday, 3rd February 19-- I attended at Oxenbury's Food Store, 44 Brunel Avenue, Fishponds, BRISTOL.
Factual detail	In the manager's office of that store I saw the Accused, LOCKE, together with Mr Ian COOPER, the store detective and Mr WILLS, the store manager.
Supportive evidence Admissible hearsay	Upon entering the office, Mr COOPER said, in the presence and hearing of the Accused, 'Earlier on today I kept this woman under observation, from the moment she entered this store, to the moment she left. During that time I saw her take from the display shelves, two pieces of steak. She did not place these items in the wire basket nor produce them for payment when she went to the check-out. She denies having the meat and has refused to allow me to search her.'
Relevant facts 'conduct of Accused'	I said to the Accused. 'You have heard what this man says, what do you say?' I cautioned LOCKE. LOCKE said, 'I haven't stolen anything'. I said, 'What is your name?' LOCKE said, 'PATRICIA LOCKE'. I said, 'Mrs LOCKE, can I look in your bag?' LOCKE said, 'If you must'.
Exhibits	I then searched a green plastic bag (ST/1) in which were the following items. One bag of flour, one bag of sugar, one packet of raisins, three bars of chocolate and a box of salt. In addition I found two pieces of steak

Signed .... S.P. TAYLOR   D.C. 1671

Exhibits

(ST/2) and (ST/3). Also in the bag I found a till receipt (ST/4).

Relevant
facts

'conduct
of Accused'

As I was doing this the Accused LOCKE said, 'Okay, so I've got the damn steak, so what'.

I said, 'I am arresting you on suspicion of stealing these two pieces of steak'.

I again cautioned LOCKE and she said, 'Okay'.

I then took LOCKE to the Fishponds Police Station.

Offence
detail
'admission

At 11.30 a.m. that same morning I again saw LOCKE in an interview room at Fishponds Police Station, in the presence of Detective Constable REDMORE.

Exhibit

I then conducted an interview of LOCKE, during which D.C. REDMORE, took contemporaneous notes (IR/1).

Signed ...... S.P. TAYLOR   D.C. 1671

STATEMENT FORM

Name .... Ian REDMORE

Address .... Avon and Somerset Constabulary, Fishponds, BRISTOL

Occupation... Detective Constable 556 .....   Age .... Over 21 years

This statement (consisting of   1   pages each signed by me) is true to the best of my knowledge and belief and I make it knowing that if it is tendered in evidence I shall be liable to prosecution if I have wilfully stated in it anything which I know to be false or do not believe to be true.

Dated the .... 3rd .. day of .. February .... 19 ....

Signed .... I. REDMORE   D.C.556

Irrelevant duplication

       I am a detective constable, in the Avon and Somerset Constabulary, currently stationed at Fishponds, BRISTOL.

Supportive evidence

       At 11.30 a.m. on Monday, 3rd February 19--, I was on duty in an interview room at the Fishponds Police Station, when D.C. TAYLOR interviewed the Accused, Patricia Mary LOCKE.

Exhibit

       I took contemporaneous notes (IR/1) of that interview.

Signed.......... I. REDMORE   D.C.556

125

INTERVIEW RECORD FORM

INTERVIEW OF .... Patricia Mary LOCKE ....

ADDRESS .... 13 Mile End Causeway, BRISTOL ....

Occupation .....Housewife.................... Date of Birth ......03.05.44.............

Interviewing Officers ...........D.C. 1671 P.S. TAYLOR...............................
                                 D.C. 556   I. REDMORE
                        ....

Other persons present ....

....

Date of Interview ....3.2.-- .... Place of Interview ..Fishponds Police Station

Time commenced ......1130 hrs............... Time concluded .....1150 hrs..................

Caution	D.C. TAYLOR	Reminded LOCKE that she was still under caution. 'Do you understand?'
	LOCKE	'Yes I do understand.'
PACE	D.C. TAYLOR	'You've been informed of your rights concerning the use of a solicitor in fact we have served a form on you giving details of the legal aid that is available.'
	LOCKE	'Yes, and I don't want a solicitor.'
Factual detail day, date, place	D.C. TAYLOR	'Earlier on this morning (3.2.--) I arrested **15 you at Oxenbury's Food Store, in Fishponds.'
	LOCKE	'Yes that's right.'
Exhibits Offence detail 'property'	D.C. TAYLOR	'Just before I arrested you I searched this green plastic bag (ST/1) and found these two pieces of steak (ST/2 and 3) inside the bag. Do you remember?'
	LOCKE	'Yes, I know you found the meat in my carrying bag, yes.'
'appropriates'	D.C. TAYLOR	'It is alleged you took these pieces of meat from the display shelves in the Oxenbury's Food Store. Did you?'
	LOCKE	'Yes I did.'
	D.C. TAYLOR	'It is further alleged you left that store without paying for these two items. Did you?'
	LOCKE	'You know I did.'
	D.C. TAYLOR	'Did you intend taking these two pieces of

(Signed) ..............P.M. LOCKE.................................

126

INTERVIEW OF Patricia Mary LOCKE   **Continuation Sheet.**

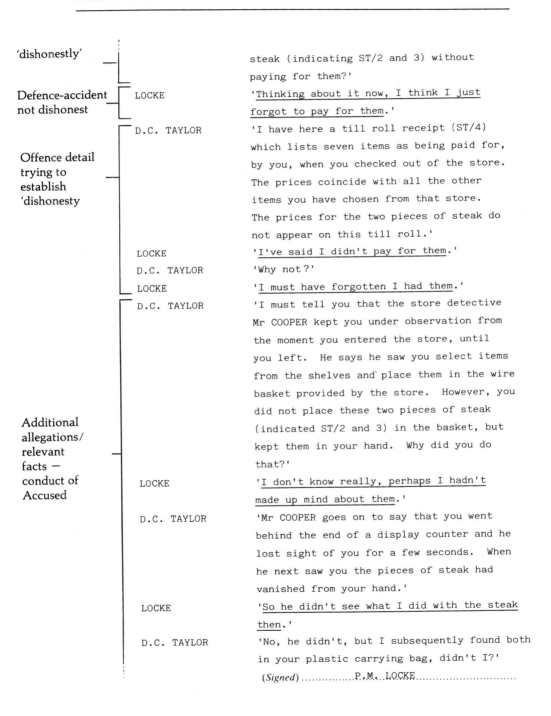

'dishonestly'

Defence-accident
not dishonest

Offence detail
trying to
establish
'dishonesty'

Additional
allegations/
relevant
facts —
conduct of
Accused

	steak (indicating ST/2 and 3) without paying for them?'
LOCKE	'Thinking about it now, I think I just forgot to pay for them.'
D.C. TAYLOR	'I have here a till roll receipt (ST/4) which lists seven items as being paid for, by you, when you checked out of the store. The prices coincide with all the other items you have chosen from that store. The prices for the two pieces of steak do not appear on this till roll.'
LOCKE	'I've said I didn't pay for them.'
D.C. TAYLOR	'Why not?'
LOCKE	'I must have forgotten I had them.'
D.C. TAYLOR	'I must tell you that the store detective Mr COOPER kept you under observation from the moment you entered the store, until you left. He says he saw you select items from the shelves and place them in the wire basket provided by the store. However, you did not place these two pieces of steak (indicated ST/2 and 3) in the basket, but kept them in your hand. Why did you do that?'
LOCKE	'I don't know really, perhaps I hadn't made up mind about them.'
D.C. TAYLOR	'Mr COOPER goes on to say that you went behind the end of a display counter and he lost sight of you for a few seconds. When he next saw you the pieces of steak had vanished from your hand.'
LOCKE	'So he didn't see what I did with the steak then.'
D.C. TAYLOR	'No, he didn't, but I subsequently found both in your plastic carrying bag, didn't I?'

(Signed) .... P.M. LOCKE ....

127

INTERVIEW OF   Patricia Mary LOCKE   **Continuation Sheet.**

	LOCKE	'You can't prove I put the steak into my bag.'
	D.C. TAYLOR	'You must have because I found them there.'
	LOCKE	'That doesn't prove I put them there, the store detective could have done it.'

Offence detail dishonest appropriation

	D.C. TAYLOR	'Mrs LOCKE, I must tell you that a witness, an ordinary member of the public, saw you when you went out of the sight of the store detective. She describes to us, how you put the two pieces of steak into this carrying bag (ST/1).'

Offence detail admission of dishonesty

	LOCKE	'Let me think for a minute' (silent for about 30 seconds). **16
		'Okay, fair enough, I did steal the damn stuff. I knew the store detective was watching me, but I thought that if I went around behind the counter he wouldn't see what I'd done. Bloody stupid really, just for five or six quid.'
	D.C. TAYLOR	'You admit then, that you stole these two pieces of steak?'
	LOCKE	'Yes I do. I suppose it's no good saying I'm sorry is it?'

Defences — negating accident

negating possible psychiatric reason

	D.C. TAYLOR	'You are not saying now, are you, that you forgot to pay for the two pieces of meat?'
	LOCKE	'No I'm not and I'm sorry I lied to you, I've been very stupid.'
	D.C. TAYLOR	'You say you've been stupid, can you tell me why, this morning, you decided to steal?'
	LOCKE	'I just thought I could get away with it, and I haven't, have I?'

	D.C. TAYLOR	'Do you wish to make a written statement about this matter?'

(Signed) .... P.M. LOCKE

INTERVIEW OF   Patricia Mary LOCKE   **Continuation Sheet.**

Written
statement

LOCKE	'I don't think so, you've been making notes and I'm sure there's nothing more to say.'
D.C. TAYLOR	'You will be released from this police station later, but I must tell you that the facts concerning this incident will be reported. Do you understand?'
LOCKE	'Yes, perfectly.'
D.C. TAYLOR	'Will you read over these notes and if you agree that they are a true record of this interview, will you sign each page?'
	LOCKE then read the notes.
LOCKE	'Yes they're correct.'
	(Signed) P.M. LOCKE
	(Signed) P.S. TAYLOR D.C. 1671
	(Signed) I. REDMORE D.C. 556

(*Signed*) ....

MESSAGE LOG

from Mr COOPER, Store Det. Oxenbury's, Fishponds

to D.C. Taylor, Fishponds CID

'I didn't have a chance to tell you earlier,
this morning, but that woman you arrested at
our store today, Mrs LOCKE, I have suspected
her for several weeks of stealing from the
store. I thought you ought to know that.'

Custody record

property

Retained by prisoner

No.	
1.	3 BARS CADBURY'S CHOCOLATE
2.	1x2lb BAG SUGAR
3.	1x2lb BAG FLOUR
4.	1 BOX SALT
5.	1 PKT RAISINS
6.	5'6 pence COIN

Certified correct

P. Locke

AVON AND SOMERSET CONSTABULARY

SURNAME   :   LOCKE
FORENAMES   :   PATRICIA
               :   MARY

OPERATOR   :   LSFCRO

URN   :   258397

CONVICTIONS   1

    1.   06-JUN-1981   COURT   : FISHPONDS
                       TYPE   : Magistrates court

              1.   OFF   :   Theft from shop
                   SENT   :   Fined £25
                              Pay £15 compensation
NNNN

Call duration: 00:00:26   Packets out: 0   Packets in: 325
*** Cleared - 0000

Report B: Road Accident

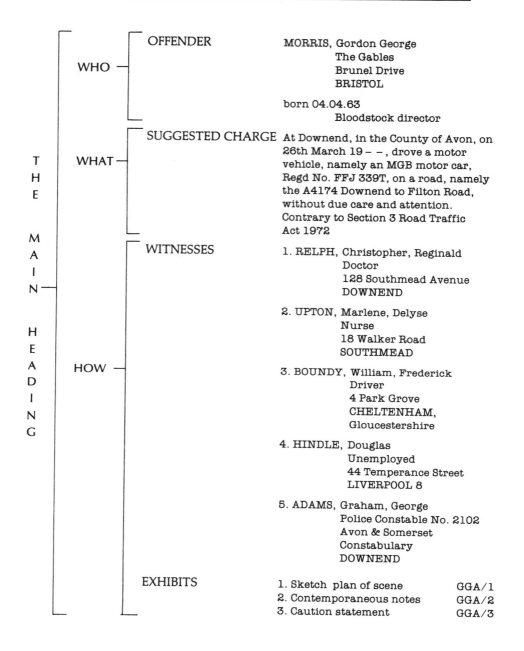

```
                      ┌── OFFENDER           MORRIS, Gordon George
                      │                            The Gables
              WHO ────┤                            Brunel Drive
                      │                            BRISTOL
                      │
                      └                       born 04.04.63
                                                   Bloodstock director

                      ┌── SUGGESTED CHARGE   At Downend, in the County of Avon, on
                      │                       26th March 19 – – , drove a motor
  T                   │                       vehicle, namely an MGB motor car,
  H           WHAT ───┤                       Regd No. FFJ 339T, on a road, namely
  E                   │                       the A4174 Downend to Filton Road,
                      │                       without due care and attention.
                      │                       Contrary to Section 3 Road Traffic
  M                   └                       Act 1972
  A
  I                   ┌── WITNESSES          1. RELPH, Christopher, Reginald
  N ──┤               │                            Doctor
                      │                            128 Southmead Avenue
                      │                            DOWNEND
  H                   │
  E                   │                      2. UPTON, Marlene, Delyse
  A                   │                            Nurse
  D           HOW ────┤                            18 Walker Road
  I                   │                            SOUTHMEAD
  N                   │
  G                   │                      3. BOUNDY, William, Frederick
                      │                            Driver
                      │                            4 Park Grove
                      │                            CHELTENHAM,
                      │                            Gloucestershire
                      │
                      │                      4. HINDLE, Douglas
                      │                            Unemployed
                      │                            44 Temperance Street
                      │                            LIVERPOOL 8
                      │
                      │                      5. ADAMS, Graham, George
                      │                            Police Constable No. 2102
                      │                            Avon & Somerset
                      │                            Constabulary
                      │                            DOWNEND
                      │
                      └── EXHIBITS           1. Sketch plan of scene         GGA/1
                                             2. Contemporaneous notes        GGA/2
                                             3. Caution statement            GGA/3
```

Sir,

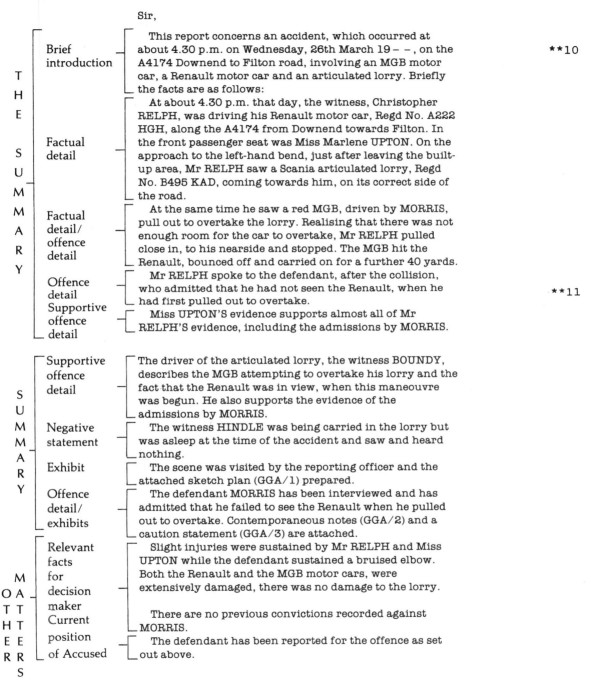

<table>
<tr><td rowspan="9">T H E S U M M A R Y</td><td>Brief introduction</td><td>This report concerns an accident, which occurred at about 4.30 p.m. on Wednesday, 26th March 19 – – , on the A4174 Downend to Filton road, involving an MGB motor car, a Renault motor car and an articulated lorry. Briefly the facts are as follows:</td><td>**10</td></tr>
</table>

THE SUMMARY

Brief introduction — This report concerns an accident, which occurred at about 4.30 p.m. on Wednesday, 26th March 19 – – , on the A4174 Downend to Filton road, involving an MGB motor car, a Renault motor car and an articulated lorry. Briefly the facts are as follows: ****10**

Factual detail — At about 4.30 p.m. that day, the witness, Christopher RELPH, was driving his Renault motor car, Regd No. A222 HGH, along the A4174 from Downend towards Filton. In the front passenger seat was Miss Marlene UPTON. On the approach to the left-hand bend, just after leaving the built-up area, Mr RELPH saw a Scania articulated lorry, Regd No. B495 KAD, coming towards him, on its correct side of the road.

Factual detail/offence detail — At the same time he saw a red MGB, driven by MORRIS, pull out to overtake the lorry. Realising that there was not enough room for the car to overtake, Mr RELPH pulled close in, to his nearside and stopped. The MGB hit the Renault, bounced off and carried on for a further 40 yards.

Offence detail — Mr RELPH spoke to the defendant, after the collision, who admitted that he had not seen the Renault, when he had first pulled out to overtake. ****11**

Supportive offence detail — Miss UPTON'S evidence supports almost all of Mr RELPH'S evidence, including the admissions by MORRIS.

THE SUMMARY

Supportive offence detail — The driver of the articulated lorry, the witness BOUNDY, describes the MGB attempting to overtake his lorry and the fact that the Renault was in view, when this maneouvre was begun. He also supports the evidence of the admissions by MORRIS.

Negative statement — The witness HINDLE was being carried in the lorry but was asleep at the time of the accident and saw and heard nothing.

Exhibit — The scene was visited by the reporting officer and the attached sketch plan (GGA/1) prepared.

Offence detail/exhibits — The defendant MORRIS has been interviewed and has admitted that he failed to see the Renault when he pulled out to overtake. Contemporaneous notes (GGA/2) and a caution statement (GGA/3) are attached.

THE OTHER MATTERS

Relevant facts for decision maker — Slight injuries were sustained by Mr RELPH and Miss UPTON while the defendant sustained a bruised elbow. Both the Renault and the MGB motor cars, were extensively damaged, there was no damage to the lorry.

There are no previous convictions recorded against MORRIS.

Current position of Accused — The defendant has been reported for the offence as set out above.

Police Constable No. 2102

135

STATEMENT FORM

Name .... Christopher Reginald RELPH

Address .... 128 Southmead Avenue, Downend, BRISTOL

Occupation ...... Medical Practitioner ...... Age ... 26 yrs (b.12.9.59)

This statement (consisting of 3 pages each signed by me) is true to the best of my knowledge and belief and I make it knowing that if it is tendered in evidence I shall be liable to prosecution if I have wilfully stated in it anything which I know to be false or do not believe to be true.

Dated the ... 26th ... day of ... March .... 19.--.. ....

Signed .... C.R. RELPH ....

Irrelevant	I am a medical practitioner, having qualified at the BRISTOL Royal Infirmary, in September 1981. I then studied at the Frenchay burns unit for two years, but since December 1983, I have been in general practice in the Downend area of BRISTOL.
Factual detail 'time, day date, place'	At 4.30 p.m. on Wednesday, 26th March 19--, I was driving my Renault 20 motor car, Regd No. A222 HGH along the Downend to Filton road, towards Filton. I had just left the Downend built-up area signs.
Relevant fact 'conduct of aggrieved'	I had just finished my home visits and had no appointments outstanding, so I was not in any particular hurry. I was just making my way back to our clinic in Filton and I suppose my speed was about 40 to 45 m.p.h., certainly no more than that. In the front passenger seat of my car was Miss Marlene UPTON, one of our nursing staff.
Factual detail 'place'	At that time we were approaching a long, left-hand bend in the road and I could see coming towards me, an articulated lorry. It was about 500 yards from me when I first saw it.
Opinion speed	It is difficult to estimate its speed, but I did not get the impression it was travelling very fast.
Offence detail 'm/v – road'	At about the same time I saw a red sports car pull out from behind the lorry. It had its right-hand indicator on and was obviously about to overtake the lorry.

Signed .... C.R. RELPH ....

Offence
detail
'careless'

> Even at that moment I knew it was almost impossible for the sports car to overtake the lorry, safely. There just wasn't enough room to get through.

Relevant
hearsay

> I remember I said, 'Christ, he's not going to make it'.

Relevant
fact
offence
detail

> I braked almost instantly and pulled in tight to my nearside.

> The lorry kept coming on and so did the sports car, which was still on my side of the road.

Opinion
'speed'
Relevant
fact

> I did not get the impression that the lorry slowed down. The sports car appeared to be speeding up.

> By this time my vehicle had virtually stopped, close in to the low bank on my nearside.

Offence
detail

> I then saw the front of the sports car dip down and I heard the sound of tyres screeching. The back end of the sports car started to come around and the car went into a skid, coming straight towards my car, broadside on.

> I saw smoke coming from the rear wheels of the lorry, the kind you see when a vehicle is under heavy braking. By this time my vehicle was stationary. I put my arms up over my face and remember seeing Miss UPTON doing the same.

**6

> An instant before I covered my face I saw the offside of the sports car collide with the front of my car. There was a very loud bang and my car was pushed back.

Relevant
fact
conduct
after offence

> After the impact both Miss UPTON and I got out of my car via the front passenger door. All the other doors were unusable. The red sports car had ended up behind my car, towards Downend.

Factual
detail
i/d offender

> Both Miss UPTON and I walked back to the sports car and as we arrived a young man began to climb out of the driver's seat. I could see that there was no one else in the car.

**7

> I said to the young man, 'What the hell were you playing at, you nearly killed us?'

Relevant facts 'conduct of Accused after offence'

He said, 'I'm sorry, I didn't see you until it was too late, the main thing is you're not injured'.

I could see that he was nursing one arm so I said, 'Are you all right, I'm a doctor'.

He said, 'I think so, although my elbow is sore. Look I'm sorry about all this, I just didn't see you when I pulled out.'

Factual detail i/d offender

I would describe the driver as 20 years, 5'10", slim build, ginger hair, cut short, clean shaven. He was wearing a check sports jacket, collar and tie and light brown cavalry twill trousers. I would definitely recognise him again.

Relevant fact/ offence detail proves accident

As a result of this accident, my car has extensive damage to most of the body shell, a cracked cyclinder head, the steering geometry is twisted and both offside wheels are damaged beyond repair.

My right knee is bruised and sore, caused at the moment of impact, when my car was pushed backwards.

Signed ........C.R. RELPH.....................

STATEMENT FORM

Name .... Marlene Delyse UPTON

Address .... 18 Walker Road, Southmead, BRISTOL

Occupation ..State Enrolled Nurse ....   Age .... 21 yrs (b.6.1.65)

This statement (consisting of 2 pages each signed by me) is true to the best of my knowledge and belief and I make it knowing that if it is tendered in evidence I shall be liable to prosecution if I have wilfully stated in it anything which I know to be false or do not believe to be true.

Dated the ....26th day of... March .... 19.--. ....

Signed........ M.D. UPTON ....

Factual detail 'time, day, date & place'	At 4.30 p.m. on Wednesday, 26th March 19--, I was riding in the front passenger seat of a Renault motor, Regd No. A222 HGH, which was being driven by Dr Christopher RELPH. At that time we were travelling out of BRISTOL, from Downend towards our surgery in Filton, along the road that links Downend to the M32 motorway. We had just left the 30 m.p.h. signs.
Opinion 'speed' Relevant fact	I would estimate our speed as a little over 30 m.p.h., we weren't going very fast. I am not a driver myself.
Factual detail	We were chatting about the day's work and, at that time, were approaching the long left-hand bend immediately before the straight that leads to the motorway.
Irrelevant hearsay	I remember Dr RELPH said, 'It's been a busy day but a most successful day, so far'.
Relevant fact Intro. details	I then saw a large blue lorry coming towards us, from the direction of Filton. It was on its correct side of the road and I didn't take much notice of it.
Opinion 'speed'	I cannot say what speed it was doing, but it didn't appear to be fast. It was about two or three hundred yards from us, when I first saw it.
Offence detail 'careless'	Just a second or two after that I saw a small red car pull out from behind the lorry and begin to overtake it.
Relevant hearsay	Dr RELPH said, '<u>Bloody idiot, he's going to hit us</u>', or '<u>He's not going to make it</u>', or words to that effect.

Signed............M.D. UPTON......................

139

Relevant fact conduct of aggrieved	He braked and our car slowed down. Dr RELPH pulled in towards the nearside bank. I could see that the red car was going quite fast and the gap between our car and it was narrowing.
Opinion	The lorry didn't seem to be altering its speed.
Offence detail 'careless'	The next thing I saw was the red car wavering in the road and I heard the screech of tyres. The front of the red car wavered from side to side and then it began to slide along the road, with its offside towards our car.
Relevant fact conduct of aggrieved	By this time our car was definitely stopped. I put my arms up to my face and then felt a tremendous bump to our car. There was a loud bang and our car moved backwards.
Negative 'statement'	Because my hands were over my eyes I cannot say what hit our car, but the last thing I saw was the red car coming towards us, still on our side of the road.
Relevant fact 'conduct after'	Both Dr RELPH and I got out of the Renault, by way of my door and we walked back towards Downend to where the red car had ended up.
Factual detail i/d offender	A youngish man got out of the red car. I could see before we arrived that he was seated in the driver's **8 seat.
Relevant fact — conduct of Accused	Dr RELPH said, 'What were you playing at', or words to that effect and I heard the young man, in the red car, say, 'I didn't see you, I'm sorry'.
Relevant fact	As a result of the accident I have a cut to my forehead and a bruise to my left shoulder.
Opinion as to why	This accident happened because the driver of the red car tried to overtake the lorry when there was not enough distance between the lorry and Dr RELPH's car for him to do so.
i/d offender	I would describe the driver of the red car as about 24 years, 5'9", slim build with short cut, reddish hair. He was smartly dressed in a sports jacket and casual trousers.
Relevant fact	I would definitely recognise him again.

Signed ..........M.D. UPTON..........

140

STATEMENT FORM

Name .... William Frederick BOUNDY ....

Address ..... 4 Park Grove, CHELTENHAM, Gloucestershire ....

Occupation. Driver.............................   Age ...47yrs. (b.18.11.38)

This statement (consisting of   3   pages each signed by me) is true to the best of my knowledge and belief and I make it knowing that if it is tendered in evidence I shall be liable to prosecution if I have wilfully stated in it anything which I know to be false or do not believe to be true.

Dated the ...26th..day of.. March .... 19.--...   ....

Signed................ W.F. BOUNDY ....

Relevant facts Intro. matters	I am employed as a driver by WALDRON, CHANNON and HOPKINS, road hauliers of CHELTENHAM and have been driving heavy lorries, both in this country and on the Continent, for the past 25 years.
Factual detail 'time, day, date and place'	At about 4.30 p.m. on Wednesday, 26th March 19--, I was driving a Scania ten-wheeled articulated lorry, Regd No. B495 KAD. I had just come off the M32 motorway, and was driving from the motorway, towards Downend, in Bristol. I had just come along the long straight, after coming off the motorway and was beginning to take the long right-hand bend that leads to the Downend shopping centre.
Relevant facts Intro. matters	My speed at that time was about 35 to 40 m.p.h. Traffic was light, the weather was fine and dry. As I was on the beginning of the bend, I could clearly see a lone car, coming towards me, from the Downend direction. It was a large blue Renault and it was about four or five hundred yards from me.
Opinion 'speed'	The Renault didn't seem to be going fast.
Offence detail 'm/veh. road'	Just then I noticed in my offside driving mirror, the right-hand indicator of a car, which had pulled out from behind my lorry. The car was a red MGB sports car. I didn't know what the driver of the red sports car intended doing, whether he was going to try to overtake

Signed............ W. F. BOUNDY ....

Offence detail	me, or turn in to a service road, off to my right, that leads to a factory.
Conduct of aggrieved	I eased off the accelerator.
	The red sports car began to overtake me.
Offence detail	I saw in my mirror that he was alongside the trailer I was pulling. At this time I was doing about 35 m.p.h.
Opinion 'speed'	and I would estimate the speed of the MGB to be only a little above that, perhaps 40 to 45 m.p.h. He was certainly taking a long time to overtake me.
Offence detail	I realised at this stage, that the Renault, coming in the other direction was getting closer and I could see that the MGB would not get by me, in time to avoid the Renault.

I immediately braked hard, keeping the trailer and my towing vehicle under control.

I saw that the Renault had pulled in tight to its nearside.

The MGB then appeared to go out of control and I saw that it was travelling broadside on, up the road, in what appeared to be a four-wheeled skid.

I was still slowing down.

The MGB slid past me and hit the Renault, which by this time was stationary and close to its nearside. The MGB hit the Renault broadside on, with its offside hitting the Renault's front bonnet.

The MGB then bounced off the Renault, narrowly missed my cab and travelled towards Downend, stopping about 40 or 50 yards past the Renault.

Relevant fact — conduct of aggrieved	I stopped my lorry just past the Renault. I saw a man and a young woman get out of the Renault and walk back to the MGB.
Factual detail i/d offender	I got out of my cab and ran to the MGB, arriving just in time to see a young man climb out of the driving seat. There was no one else in the MGB.

I heard the driver of the Renault say, to the driver of the MGB, 'What the hell do you think you were playing at, you nearly killed us?'

Signed .... W.F. BOUNDY

142

Admissible hearsay Supportive (RELPH) and conduct of Accused

The young man, from the MGB said, 'I'm sorry, I didn't see you'.

I heard the Renault driver say something about being a doctor and the driver of the MGB said, again, 'I'm sorry, I just didn't see you'.

Relevant fact

I have no injuries and there is no damage to either my truck or the trailer.

Opinion as to WHY

This accident happened because the driver of the MGB totally misjudged his overtaking of my lorry.

Factual detail i/d offender

I would describe the driver of the MGB as being in his early 20s, about 5'9", slim build, very striking ginger hair, cut short. He was wearing a sports jacket and casual trousers and I would definitely recognise him again.

Relevant fact

I would add that at the time of this accident I had a passenger in my cab, a hitch-hiker I had picked up at the Birmingham Service Station. I believe he was asleep at the time of the accident.

Signed .... W.F. BOUNDY ....

143

STATEMENT FORM

Name .... Douglas HINDLE ....

Address .... 44 Temperance Street, LIVERPOOL ....

Occupation... Unemployed ....   Age 19 yrs (b 9.9.66).

This statement (consisting of   2   pages each signed by me) is true to the best of my knowledge and belief and I make it knowing that if it is tendered in evidence I shall be liable to prosecution if I have wilfully stated in it anything which I know to be false or do not believe to be true.

Dated the .. 26th ... day of .... March .... 19 .‑‑..   ....

Signed .... D. HINDLE ....

Irrelevant	I am an unemployed hotel worker, having been previously employed in large hotels, as a kitchen porter, in the North of England. Since June 19-- I have been unemployed.
Relevant facts Intro. matters	At about 2.0 p.m. on Wednesday, 26th March, 19-- I was in one of the service stations, south of Birmingham, on the M5 motorway, when I managed to get a lift in a large articulated lorry, Regd No. B495 KAD, which was travelling to the West country. After we left the service station I chatted with the driver for about 15 minutes, then I went to sleep. The next thing I knew was the lorry coming to a sudden halt, which woke me up.
Relevant hearsay	The driver said, 'There's been an accident'.
Negative 'statement'	At that time we were in the outskirts of the city of BRISTOL. I have been asked if I saw anything of this accident and I can say I did not, I was asleep. I have been asked if I can give any details of the speed of the lorry and I cannot. I have been asked if I can give any details about a red MGB sports car and its overtaking of the lorry and I cannot. After I woke up I stayed in the cab of the lorry and did not see any of the other drivers involved, neither did I hear any conversation between any of the drivers,

Signed .... D. HINDLE ....

144

Negative 'statement'

concerning the accident.

I have been asked if I can give any details about a Renault motor car, which apparently was involved in this accident, and I cannot, I was asleep.

Relevant fact

I have no injuries as a result of this accident.

STATEMENT FORM

Name ... Graham George ADAMS

Address ... Avon and Somerset Constabulary, Downend, BRISTOL

Occupation ... Police Constable 2102   Age ... Over 21 Years

This statement (consisting of 2 pages each signed by me) is true to the best of my knowledge and belief and I make it knowing that if it is tendered in evidence I shall be liable to prosecution if I have wilfully stated in it anything which I know to be false or do not believe to be true.

Dated the ..26th.... day of .... March .... 19--...   ....

Signed ...... G.G.ADAMS ....

Irrelevant	I am a Police Constable of the Avon and Somerset Constabulary, currently stationed at Downend, BRISTOL.
Factual detail 'day, date, place'	At about 4.45 p.m. on Wednesday, 26th March 19-- I was on duty, when I attended the scene of a road accident on the A4174 Downend to Filton road, involving a Scania articulated lorry, an MGB sports car and a Renault motor car.
Factual/offence detail i/d offender 'driver'	At the scene I spoke to the defendant, Gordon George MORRIS. I said, 'Are you driver of the MGB sports car, Regd No. FFJ 339T?' MORRIS said 'Yes, I am'.
Relevant fact	I cautioned him and said, 'Have any of the vehicles, involved in this accident, been moved, since the accident?' MORRIS said, 'No, they are exactly as they were'.
Exhibit	With the assistance of MORRIS and a Mr William BOUNDY I then took measurements of the scene, from which I prepared a sketch (GGA/1).
Relevant facts	I further noted that the weather was fine and the road surface dry, at the time of my examination of the scene.
Offence detail 'admission' Exhibit	At 8.50 p.m. that same day I again saw MORRIS in an interview room at the Downend Police Station. Throughout the whole of that interview I took a contemporaneous note (GGA/2).

Signed ...... G.G. ADAMS   P.C. 2102 ....

146

xhibit

        Towards the end of the interview MORRIS elected to make a written statement under caution (GGA/3) which I wrote at his dictation.

INTERVIEW RECORD FORM

INTERVIEW OF .... Gordon George MORRIS ....

ADDRESS .... The Gables, Brunel Drive, BRISTOL ....

Occupation ..... Bloodstock director ..... Date of Birth ...... 04.04.63 ....

Interviewing Officers ..... P.C. 2102   G.G. ADAMS ....

....

Other persons present ....

....

Date of Interview .... 26.3.-- ....   Place of Interview ... Downend Police Station

Time commenced .... 2050 hrs ....   Time concluded ...... 2120 hrs ....

Caution	P.C. ADAMS	Cautioned MORRIS. 'Do you understand?'
	MORRIS	'I understand, carry on.'
PACE	P.C. ADAMS	'Do you wish to have a solicitor present during this interview?'
	MORRIS	'That won't be necessary.'
	P.C. ADAMS	'You realise you may, at any time, leave this police station?'
	MORRIS	'Yes, of course, but I do understand that we have to talk about the accident and I would like to sort it out as quickly as possible.'
Factual detail establishing 'time, day, place'	P.C. ADAMS	'I am investigating the circumstances surrounding an accident that happened on the A4174 Downend to Filton road, at about 4.40 p.m. today, involving your car, which is an MGB sports car, a Renault motor car and an articulated lorry. Do you understand?'
	MORRIS	'Yes, I do.'
Offence detail establishing 'driver'	P.C. ADAMS	'You may recall I saw you at the scene of the accident earlier today and you told me that you were driving the MGB sports car, Regd No. FFJ 339T. Is that right, were you the driver of that vehicle?'
	MORRIS	'Yes, I was.'
	P.C. ADAMS	'And is it right that at about 4.30 p.m.

(Signed) .... G.G. MORRIS ....

INTERVIEW OF Gordon George MORRIS   **Continuation Sheet.**

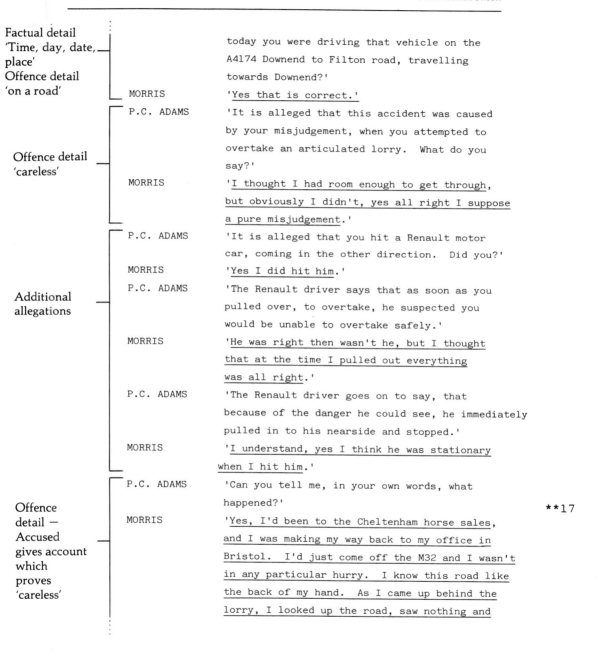

Factual detail 'Time, day, date, place' **Offence detail** 'on a road'		'today you were driving that vehicle on the A4174 Downend to Filton road, travelling towards Downend?'
	MORRIS	'Yes that is correct.'
	P.C. ADAMS	'It is alleged that this accident was caused by your misjudgement, when you attempted to overtake an articulated lorry. What do you say?'
Offence detail 'careless'	MORRIS	'I thought I had room enough to get through, but obviously I didn't, yes all right I suppose a pure misjudgement.'
	P.C. ADAMS	'It is alleged that you hit a Renault motor car, coming in the other direction. Did you?'
	MORRIS	'Yes I did hit him.'
	P.C. ADAMS	'The Renault driver says that as soon as you pulled over, to overtake, he suspected you would be unable to overtake safely.'
Additional allegations	MORRIS	'He was right then wasn't he, but I thought that at the time I pulled out everything was all right.'
	P.C. ADAMS	'The Renault driver goes on to say, that because of the danger he could see, he immediately pulled in to his nearside and stopped.'
	MORRIS	'I understand, yes I think he was stationary when I hit him.'
	P.C. ADAMS	'Can you tell me, in your own words, what happened?'
Offence detail — Accused gives account which proves 'careless'	MORRIS	'Yes, I'd been to the Cheltenham horse sales, and I was making my way back to my office in Bristol. I'd just come off the M32 and I wasn't in any particular hurry. I know this road like the back of my hand. As I came up behind the lorry, I looked up the road, saw nothing and

**17

(*Signed*) ...G.G. MORRIS...

149

INTERVIEW OF Gordon George MORRIS   **Continuation Sheet.**

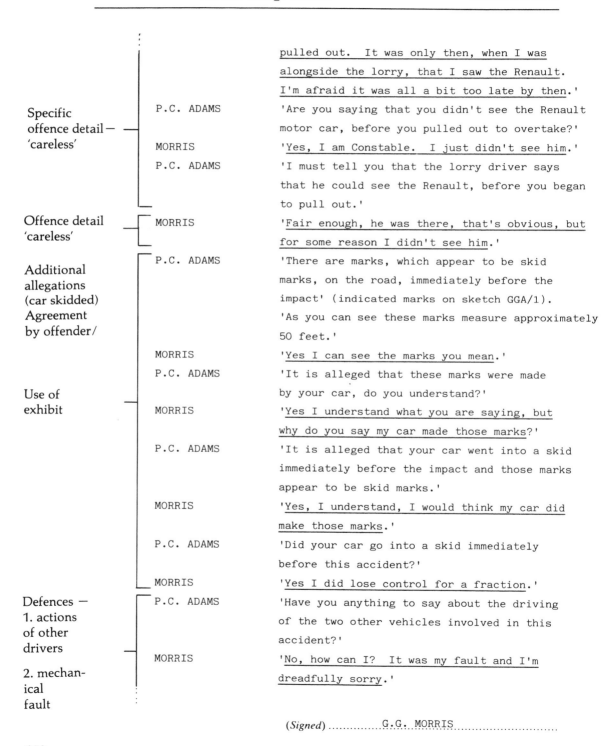

Specific offence detail — 'careless'		
		pulled out. It was only then, when I was alongside the lorry, that I saw the Renault. I'm afraid it was all a bit too late by then.'
	P.C. ADAMS	'Are you saying that you didn't see the Renault motor car, before you pulled out to overtake?'
	MORRIS	'Yes, I am Constable. I just didn't see him.'
	P.C. ADAMS	'I must tell you that the lorry driver says that he could see the Renault, before you began to pull out.'

Offence detail 'careless'

MORRIS — 'Fair enough, he was there, that's obvious, but for some reason I didn't see him.'

Additional allegations (car skidded) Agreement by offender/

P.C. ADAMS — 'There are marks, which appear to be skid marks, on the road, immediately before the impact' (indicated marks on sketch GGA/1). 'As you can see these marks measure approximately 50 feet.'

MORRIS — 'Yes I can see the marks you mean.'

P.C. ADAMS — 'It is alleged that these marks were made by your car, do you understand?'

Use of exhibit

MORRIS — 'Yes I understand what you are saying, but why do you say my car made those marks?'

P.C. ADAMS — 'It is alleged that your car went into a skid immediately before the impact and those marks appear to be skid marks.'

MORRIS — 'Yes, I understand, I would think my car did make those marks.'

P.C. ADAMS — 'Did your car go into a skid immediately before this accident?'

MORRIS — 'Yes I did lose control for a fraction.'

Defences —
1. actions of other drivers

P.C. ADAMS — 'Have you anything to say about the driving of the two other vehicles involved in this accident?'

MORRIS — 'No, how can I? It was my fault and I'm dreadfully sorry.'

2. mechanical fault

(*Signed*) .... G.G. MORRIS ....

INTERVIEW OF   Gordon George MORRIS   **Continuation Sheet.**

P.C. ADAMS	'Your car is a 'T' registration. Is it mechanically sound?'
MORRIS	'Yes, it's in tip top condition. I can show you the garage bills if you like.'
P.C. ADAMS	'You are saying now that this accident was caused by a pure misjudgement on your part, when you overtook the lorry.'
MORRIS	'Yes, that's what happened.'
P.C. ADAMS	'You can, if you wish make a written statement about this matter. Do you wish to do so?'
MORRIS	'Yes, I would like to do that.'
P.C. ADAMS	'Do you wish to write it yourself or shall I take it down at your dictation?'
MORRIS	'I'll dictate it to you, if you don't mind.'
2105 hrs	Statement commenced.
2115 hrs	Statement ceased.
P.C. ADAMS	'You will be reported for the offence of driving a motor vehicle on a road, without due care and attention.'
MORRIS	'I do understand and I'm sorry for what has happened.'
P. C. ADAMS	'Will you now read these notes and, if you agree them to be a correct record of the interview, would you sign each page, please?'
MORRIS	'Certainly.'
	Notes read by MORRIS
MORRIS	'Yes that's exactly how it went.'

Written statement _(bracket marking the written statement section)_

(Signed) G.G. MORRIS
(Signed) G.G. ADAMS   P.C. 2102

(*Signed*) ....

151

Division ....

Station .... Downend ....

Date .... 26th March 19-- ......

Statement of .Gordon George MORRIS ....

Address .... The Gables, Brunel Drive, BRISTOL ....

Date of Birth .04.04.63.....................   Place of Birth .....BRISTOL................

Occupation ...Director of Bloodstock company.......................................

CAUTION

I, ...Gordon George MORRIS ....
wish to make a statement. I want someone to write down what I say. I understand that I need not
say anything unless I wish to do so and that what I say may be given in evidence.

................(Signed) G.G. MORRIS ....

Signature of person making statement

2105 hrs   I would just like to say that I am sorry
            for what happened today (26.3.--) by that I mean the
            accident involving my car and the Renault car, on the road
            near Downend. It was totally my fault and I just didn't see
            the other car at the moment I pulled out to overtake. I saw
            it too late, braked, lost control and my car just slid into
            the Renault. I haven't got any injuries and I understand the
            other people involved are not seriously injured, and for that
            I am most relieved. I can only apologise for what must have
            been a temporary lapse in my concentration. I have read the
            above statement and I have been able to correct, alter or add
            anything I wish. This statement is true. I have made it of
            my own free will. (Signed) G.G. MORRIS
                         Statement taken and signature witnessed by
            the undersigned at Downend Police Station on Wednesday,
2115 hrs   26th March 19--. (Signed) G.G. ADAMS   P.C. 2102

152

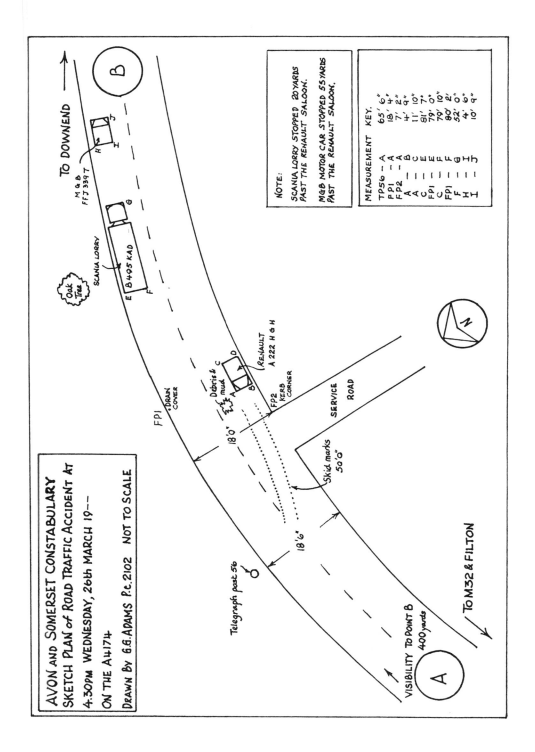

AVON and SOMERSET CONSTABULARY
SKETCH PLAN of ROAD TRAFFIC ACCIDENT AT
4.30PM WEDNESDAY, 26th MARCH 19——
ON THE A4174
DRAWN BY G.G. ADAMS P.c. 2102   NOT TO SCALE

TO DOWNEND →

M&B
FFJ 339T

Oak
Tree

SCANIA LORRY

E B405 KAD

FP1

DRAIN
COVER

Debris &
mud

RENAULT
A 222 H&H

FP2
KERB
CORNER

18'0"

18'6"

SKID MARKS
50'0"

SERVICE
ROAD

Telegraph post 56

VISIBILITY TO POINT B
400 yards

A

To M32 & FILTON

NOTE:
SCANIA LORRY STOPPED 20 YARDS
PAST THE RENAULT SALOON.

M&B MOTOR CAR STOPPED 55 YARDS
PAST THE RENAULT SALOON.

MEASUREMENT KEY.
TP56 – A   65' 6"
FP1 – A   18' 4"
FP2 – A   7' 2"
A – B   4' 9"
C – E   11' 10"
E – F   81' 7"
FP1 – F   79' 0"
C – F   79' 10"
FP1 – F   80' 2"
F – G   52' 0"
H – I   4' 6"
I – J   10' 9"

ACCIDENT
REPORT

DAMAGE
TO

Vehicle 1   MGB motor car Regd No. FFJ 339T

Front of car, nearside and offside front

extensively dented and twisted. Both

doors buckled, chassis twisted, engine

cracked, front wheels out of alignment.

Vehicle 2   Renault motor car, Regd No. A222 HGH

Body shell twisted, cracked cylinder

head, steering geometry twisted, offside

front and rear wheels destroyed.

REQUEST FOR CONVICTIONS

ILE NAME : MORRIS/GORDON GEORGE
AME CHARGED/SUMMONSED : MORRIS /GORDON GEORGE
RO NO : N/T
AIDEN NAME : --
_IAS(ES) : --
OB : 040463 SEX : MALE
DENTITY CODE : 1
EIGHT : 5 11   BORN : CHELTENHAM
URRENT ADDRESS : "THE GABLES" BRUNEL DRIVE, BRISTOL.
EASON FOR REQUEST : REPORTED
RREST/SUMMON TIME + DATE : REPORTED
PPEARING AT : FILTON MAGISTRATES
OURT + DATE : TO BE DECIDED.
AIL OR CUSTODY : REPORTED
FFENCE(S) : CARELESS DRIVING

IC : P.C 2102 ADAMS
TATION CODE : FG11
NNN

all duration: 00:00:17   Packets out: 0   Packets in: 188
** Cleared - 0000

URNAME   : MORRIS
ORENAMES   : GORDON
                    : GEORGE

PERATOR   : QRFSUP

RN   : 048712

ONVICTIONS   0

NNN

all duration: 00:00:18   Packets out: 0   Packets in: 223
** Cleared - 0000

Report C: Grievous Bodily Harm

```
┌─ WHO ──┬─ OFFENDER            HURFORD, Malcolm Phillip
│        │                          101 Egremont Terrace
│        │                          LEEDS   Yorkshire
│        │
│        │                          born 14.4.64
│        │                          Labourer
│ WHAT ──┼─ STANDS CHARGED      At LEEDS in the County of Yorkshire,
│        │                      on the 31st day of May 19 – –
│        │                      unlawfully and maliciously inflicted
│        │                      grievous bodily harm, on Terence
│        │                      PATTINSON.
│        │                      Contrary to Section 20 of the Offences
│        └                      Against the Persons Act 1861
│        ┌─ WITNESSES           1. PATTINSON, Terence James
│        │                              Bank clerk
│        │                              18 Verity Road
│        │                              LEEDS   Yorks
│        │
│        │                      2. OAKDEN, Graham
│        │                              Carpenter
│        │                              118 The Avenue
│        │                              Moss Lane
│        │                              LEEDS   Yorks
│        │
│        │                      3. GRIGG, William Alfred
│        │                              Bricklayer
│        │                              115 The Avenue
│        │                              Moss Lane
│        │                              LEEDS   Yorks
│ HOW ──┤                       4. DENSHAM, Peter Lloyd
│        │                              Doctor
│        │                              The Old School House
│        │                              Sefton Lane
│        │                              LEEDS   Yorks
│        │
│        │                      5. RICHARDS, Martin
│        │                              Detective Constable 55
│        │                              West Yorkshire
│        │                              Constabulary
└        └                              LEEDS   Yorks
```

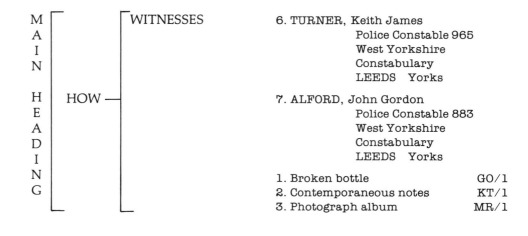

```
M ┌      ┌ WITNESSES        6. TURNER, Keith James
A │      │                       Police Constable 965
I │      │                       West Yorkshire
N │      │                       Constabulary
  │      │                       LEEDS   Yorks
H │ HOW ─┤                 7. ALFORD, John Gordon
E │      │                       Police Constable 883
A │      │                       West Yorkshire
D │      │                       Constabulary
I │      │                       LEEDS   Yorks
N │      │
G │      │                 1. Broken bottle            GO/1
  └      └                 2. Contemporaneous notes    KT/1
                           3. Photograph album         MR/1
```

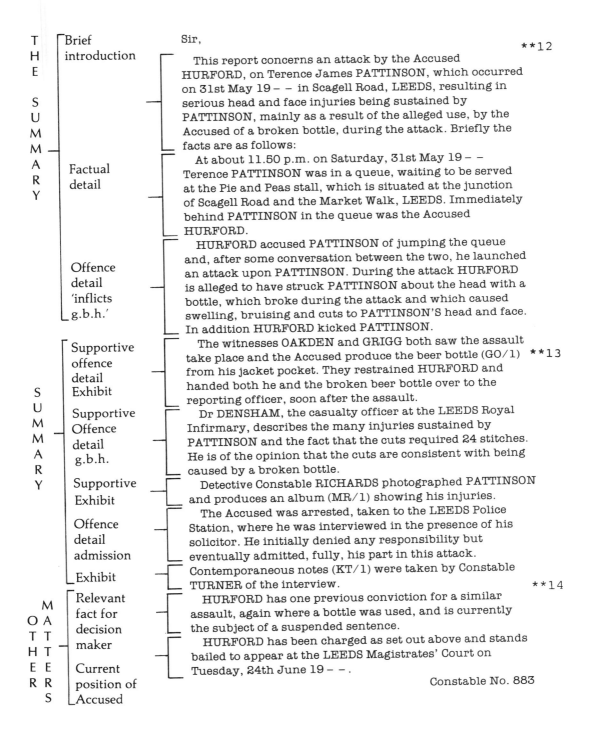

Sir,   **12

**12

THE SUMMARY

Brief introduction

This report concerns an attack by the Accused HURFORD, on Terence James PATTINSON, which occurred on 31st May 19 – – in Scagell Road, LEEDS, resulting in serious head and face injuries being sustained by PATTINSON, mainly as a result of the alleged use, by the Accused of a broken bottle, during the attack. Briefly the facts are as follows:

Factual detail

At about 11.50 p.m. on Saturday, 31st May 19 – – Terence PATTINSON was in a queue, waiting to be served at the Pie and Peas stall, which is situated at the junction of Scagell Road and the Market Walk, LEEDS. Immediately behind PATTINSON in the queue was the Accused HURFORD.

Offence detail 'inflicts g.b.h.'

HURFORD accused PATTINSON of jumping the queue and, after some conversation between the two, he launched an attack upon PATTINSON. During the attack HURFORD is alleged to have struck PATTINSON about the head with a bottle, which broke during the attack and which caused swelling, bruising and cuts to PATTINSON'S head and face. In addition HURFORD kicked PATTINSON.

SUMMARY

Supportive offence detail Exhibit

The witnesses OAKDEN and GRIGG both saw the assault take place and the Accused produce the beer bottle (GO/1) **13 from his jacket pocket. They restrained HURFORD and handed both he and the broken beer bottle over to the reporting officer, soon after the assault.

Supportive Offence detail g.b.h.

Dr DENSHAM, the casualty officer at the LEEDS Royal Infirmary, describes the many injuries sustained by PATTINSON and the fact that the cuts required 24 stitches. He is of the opinion that the cuts are consistent with being caused by a broken bottle.

Supportive Exhibit

Detective Constable RICHARDS photographed PATTINSON and produces an album (MR/1) showing his injuries.

Offence detail admission

The Accused was arrested, taken to the LEEDS Police Station, where he was interviewed in the presence of his solicitor. He initially denied any responsibility but eventually admitted, fully, his part in this attack.

Exhibit

Contemporaneous notes (KT/1) were taken by Constable TURNER of the interview.   **14

OTHERS / MATTERS

Relevant fact for decision maker

HURFORD has one previous conviction for a similar assault, again where a bottle was used, and is currently the subject of a suspended sentence.

Current position of Accused

HURFORD has been charged as set out above and stands bailed to appear at the LEEDS Magistrates' Court on Tuesday, 24th June 19 – – .

Constable No. 883

**13
**14

STATEMENT FORM

Name ..... Terence James PATTINSON

Address ..... 18 Verity Road, South Bank, LEEDS, Yorkshire

Occupation ..... Bank Clerk ..... Age ..... 19 yrs (b.16.6.66)

This statement (consisting of 4 pages each signed by me) is true to the best of my knowledge and belief and I make it knowing that if it is tendered in evidence I shall be liable to prosecution if I have wilfully stated in it anything which I know to be false or do not believe to be true.

Dated the ..... 1st ..... day of ..... June ..... 19 ..... --

Signed ..... T.J. PATTINSON

Irrelevant repetition

I am a bank clerk, currently employed by the National Bank and I am due soon to take up a more senior position, with the company, at a branch in SHEFFIELD.

Factual detail 'time, day, date, place'

At about 11.50 p.m. on Saturday, 31st May 19-- I was on my way home, when I decided to stop for some take-away food.

At that time I joined a queue of people, waiting to be served at the Pie and Peas stall, which is situated at the junction of Scagell Road and Market Walk, LEEDS.

Relevant facts Intro. matters

I joined the end of the queue, which at that time consisted of about six people, stretching back from the stall, towards Market Walk.

The queue was moving quite quickly and very soon I was about third. By this time four or five other people had arrived and were behind me in the queue.

Relevant facts conduct of Accused

At this time, the man immediately behind, said to me, 'You're jumping the queue mate, get back where you belong'.

This man was one of those who had joined the queue after I had arrived and had stood behind me for about two minutes.

Conduct of victim Conduct of Accused

I said to him, 'I think you've got it wrong, I was here before you, I haven't jumped the queue'.

The man said, 'You bloody well have, you shit, I won't tell you again, bugger off to the back'.

Signed ..... T.J. PATTINSON

160

Relevant
facts
Conduct of
Accused

          I could smell intoxicating liquor on the
man's breath and his speech was slightly slurred, but
I didn't get the impression that he was drunk.

Opinion

          The man just seemed belligerent and I got the
impression he wanted to pick a fight with me.

Conduct of
victim

          I said, 'You've got it wrong, I'm not moving,
so let's leave it at that'. I then turned away from
the man and looked towards the front of the queue.

Conduct of
Accused

          I then heard the man say, 'Don't turn your
back on me mate'.

          I turned around again and this time I could
see the man was holding a beer bottle in his hand. I
can't be sure, but I think it was a Newcastle Brown
Ale bottle.

Conduct of
victim

          I then started to say, 'Look, this is ridiculous,
we're only waiting for some pie and peas'.

          The man interrupted me and said, 'Right you've
asked for it'.

          He then lunged at me, pushing the bottle at
me.

Offence
detail
'assault'

          He was holding the bottle by its neck, in his
right hand and he pushed the bottle straight at my face.

          I was hit on my right cheek by the bottle and
at the same time I began to fall to my left.

Grievous
bodily
harm

          I grabbed hold of the man, who was attacking
me, by the lapels of his jacket, in an effort to regain
my balance.

          He hit me again with the bottle, this time
on the right temple and the bottle broke as it hit me.

          He then jabbed the broken bottle into my cheek.

Defences

He did this quite deliberately.

Relevant
facts
Conduct of
Accused

          All the while he was swearing and calling me
abusive names. I cannot be precise about everything
that he said, but I remember such phrases as, 'You bastard
I'm going to do you' and 'I'll kill you, you bastard'.

Conduct of
Victim
Offence
detail

          In order to defend myself I hit out at the
man, catching him on the shoulder, with my fist. At
the same time he kicked at me, hitting me in the stomach.

Signed .... T.J. PATTINSON

161

Offence detail

> I began to fall to the ground.
>
> The man then hit me with his knee, in my face, and I was knocked backwards and to the ground.

Relevant facts Conduct of Accused after offence

> The man then lunged towards me, still holding the bottle in his right hand. He was pushing it towards me like a man with a sword would lunge, but at that moment   ****5** I saw two men grab him by his arms and hold him.
>
> He was still shouting and I heard him say, <u>'Leave go of me, I'll kill the bastard'</u>.
>
> He was struggling violently, kicking out and twisting in an attempt to free himself.
>
> Then the police arrived and I saw the man taken away to a police car.

Offence detail proving injuries g.b.h.

> I was taken to the LEEDS Royal Infirmary, where I was treated for my injuries, which consist of the following.
>
> A bruised and swollen right cheek, a large bruise and a lump on my right temple, a series of deep cuts to my left cheek requiring 24 stitches and bruising to my ribs and stomach.
>
> I have experienced headaches and pains to my face since this attack and have been signed off work for the next three weeks.

Defence

> I had never before seen the man who attacked me.

Factual detail i/d offender

> I would describe him as being about my age, 20 to 22 years old, 5'11" tall, well-built, with very wide shoulders, dark brown collar length hair, a full moustache and sideburns. He spoke with a pronounced Northern accent, I think it might have been Lancashire, although I cannot be sure. He was wearing blue jeans, an open necked shirt and light brown leather jacket.
>
> I would definitely recognise him again.
>
> The man who assaulted me was the man I saw being led away by the police.

Defence

> This attack took place in exactly the manner I have described. It was completely unprovoked and I cannot think of any reason for the man attacking me in this manner.

Signed ............T.J. PATTINSON............

STATEMENT OF   Terence James PATTINSON   **Continuation Sheet**

Conduct of victim/ defences

I did hit the man, once, during this attack, but this was in self-defence, although it seemed to make very little difference to the man.

The occasion I hit him was as I have previously described, with my fist to his shoulder.

Signed .... T.J. PATTINSON 163

STATEMENT FORM

Name .... Graham OAKDEN

Address ...... 118 The Avenue, Moss Lane, LEEDS, Yorkshire

Occupation .. Carpenter   Age .. 25 yrs (b.28.8.60)

This statement (consisting of   4   pages each signed by me) is true to the best of my knowledge and belief and I make it knowing that if it is tendered in evidence I shall be liable to prosecution if I have wilfully stated in it anything which I know to be false or do not believe to be true.

Dated the ... 1st ... day of ..... June .... 19 ---- ....

Signed .... G. OAKDEN

Factual detail 'time, day, date, place'	At about 11.50 p.m. on Saturday, 31st May, 19--, I was in a queue of people waiting to be served at the Pie and Peas stall, in Scagell Road, near the junction with Market Walk, LEEDS.
I/D of offender	There were about six or seven people in front of me, in the queue and immediately behind me was my friend William GRIGG. There was a man immediately in front of me and he was wearing a lightish coloured leather jacket.
Relevant facts Conduct of Accused	I was talking to William about football, when I heard the man in front, say something like, 'You've been bloody queue jumping mate', or words to that effect. He appeared to be talking to the person immediately in front of him, another young man, who was wearing a sports jacket. I can say right now that there had been no queue jumping, as the man in the leather coat took his place in the queue only seconds before we did and by that time the young man in the sports jacket was already in the queue.
Conduct of victim	The young man said something like, 'No I haven't', or 'I think you're mistaken', or something like that, but the man in the leather jacket kept arguing.
Conduct of Accused Opinion WHY	I remember the man in the leather jacket was swearing a lot, but I can't be more precise than that. I got the impression he was trying to stir things up and cause trouble.
Relevant fact	By this time William and I were watching what was going on.

Signed .... G. OAKDEN

164

Conduct of victim

The young man in the sports jacket, turned away and looked to his front.

Offence detail

The man in the leather jacket said, '<u>Don't turn your back on me</u>' and then I saw him take a bottle from his jacket pocket.

It was an empty Newcastle Brown Ale bottle.

He was gripping the bottle by the neck.

I heard him say, '<u>You've asked for it</u>', and I saw him hit the young man in the face with the bottle.

He hit him again, on the top of the head and I saw the bottle break. Then I saw the man in the leather jacket jab the broken bottle into the young man's face.

Defence (disproving accident)

It was a deliberate jab, it was not done accidentally. From what I could see it was intended.

Defence (disproving self-defence)

The young man was trying to defend himself, but I cannot say whether he struck the man in the leather jacket, or not. I don't recall seeing a blow struck, but I cannot be sure on that.

Offence detail

I began to move forward to stop the fight and as I did so the man in the leather jacket kicked the young man in the stomach and then, as the young man doubled up, kneed him in the face.

Relevant facts Conduct of Accused

While he was doing all this, the man in the leather jacket was swearing and shouting, saying such things as '<u>I'll get you, you bastard</u>'.

I grabbed hold of the right hand of the man, which still held the broken bottle and, as I did so, WILLIAM grabbed hold of his left hand.

The man was struggling violently and I had to hold on tight to stop him getting away. He was still kicking out with his feet, towards the young man, on the ground, and trying to get to the young man.

He was shouting out such things as, '<u>Let me go you bastards, let me get at him</u>'.

We held on to him, however, and, within seconds, or so it seemed, a police officer arrived.

Signed ....   G. OAKDEN

165

**Relevant
fact
Admissible
hearsay**

I said to the police officer, within the hearing of the man in the leather jacket, who was still in my grasp, 'This man has just attacked that man, with a bottle'. I indicated, as I spoke, to the young man lying on the ground.

I said, 'It looked a totally senseless thing to do'.

**Supportive
(ALFORD)**

The Constable said to the man in the leather jacket, 'I am arresting you on suspicion of causing grievous bodily harm'.

The Constable then told the man that anything he said would be given in evidence, or something like that.

The man said, 'It was self-defence Constable, just self-defence'.

The Constable said, 'Where's the bottle?'

The man said, 'Bottle, what bottle? I didn't have any bottle'.

A second Constable arrived then and they took the man to a nearby police car.

**Exhibit
(finding it
tends to
support victim)**

When they did this I searched around and, quite close to the man on the ground, I found the broken bottle (GO/1) that the man had used in the attack.

**Admissible
hearsay**

I took the bottle over to the police car and in the presence and hearing of the man in the leather jacket I said, 'Here's the bottle Constable, he must have dropped it when he saw you'. I handed the bottle to the first Constable who had arrived at the fight.

The man in the leather jacket said, 'Nothing to do with me mate'.

**Supportive
(ALFORD)
Reason why**

I cannot say why this assault took place, there seemed to be no reason for it at all.

**Defences
(disproves
provacation and
self-defence)**

I can say that the young man in the sports jacket did nothing that I could see to provoke this fight.

I did not see the young man in the sports jacket hit the man in the leather jacket.

166

Signed .... G. OAKDEN ....

Relevant
facts
conduct of
Accused

> I have been asked if either of the two men involved in this fight had been drinking. I can definitely say that the man in the leather jacket had been drinking. He smelt strongly of drink.

Opinion

> However, having said that, I did not get the impression that he was drunk.

Relevant
fact conduct
of victim

> I cannot say about the injured man, but he did not give the impression of being drunk or under the influence of drink.

Factual
detail
i/d
offender

> I would describe the man in the leather jacket as being about 20 to 25 years, 6'0" tall, very well built, dark collar length hair, with a moustache. He was wearing jeans and a pale coloured leather jacket. He spoke with a Lancashire accent.
>
> I would definitely recognise him again.

STATEMENT FORM

Name .... William Alfred GRIGG

Address .... 115 The Avenue, Moss Lane, LEEDS, Yorkshire

Occupation.... Bricklayer .... Age .... 24 yrs (b.1.9.61)

This statement (consisting of 3 pages each signed by me) is true to the best of my knowledge and belief and I make it knowing that if it is tendered in evidence I shall be liable to prosecution if I have wilfully stated in it anything which I know to be false or do not believe to be true.

Dated the..... 1st ..day of....... June .... 19. ---- . ...

Signed................. W.A. GRIGG ....

<table>
<tr><td>

Factual details 'time, day, date, place'

</td><td>

    At 11.50 p.m. on Saturday, 31st May 19-- I was with my friend Graham OAKDEN, in a queue of people, waiting at the Pie and Peas stall, at the junction of Scagell Road and Market Walk, LEEDS.
    There were about four or five people in front of us.

</td></tr>
<tr><td>

Relevant facts conduct of Accused

</td><td>

    Graham and I were having a chat, when I heard the man in front of Graham start shouting. I cannot be more precise but I think he said, 'You're in my place mate', or, 'You've jumped the queue', or something like that.

</td></tr>
<tr><td>

Factual detail i/d offender

</td><td>

    The man, who was wearing a yellowish leather jacket, was talking to a man immediately in front of him. This second man was quite smartly dressed in a light coloured sports jacket.

</td></tr>
<tr><td>

Relevant facts Conduct of Accused victim

</td><td>

    There was some discussion between the two men and although I cannot remember exactly what was said, it was obvious that the man in the leather jacket was causing a disturbance. I say this because he was raising his voice and swearing and shouting, while the other man was talking quietly and I didn't hear him swearing.

</td></tr>
<tr><td>

Offence detail

</td><td>

    Suddenly I saw the man in the leather jacket take an empty beer bottle from a jacket pocket. I can't say for sure, but I think he held it in his right hand. I remember he said, something like, 'You've asked for it'. or 'You've asked for this'.

</td></tr>
</table>

Signed....................... W.A. GRIGG ....

168

Offence detail 'assault' 'g.b.h.'

He then hit the man in the sports jacket, several times to the head. It was definitely three or four blows, certainly no more than four I would say.

The blows were to the face and to the top of the head and he used the bottle as a weapon on each of the blows.

On one of the blows the bottle smashed and the man in the leather jacket then pushed the broken neck of the bottle into the face of the other man. I also saw him kick the other man. He kicked him in the groin, I thought, because the man in the sports jacket doubled over and began to fall to the ground. As he did so the man in the leather jacket caught him with his knee, in his face.

Relevant facts Conduct of Accused after offence

Graham and I moved in then and grabbed the man in the leather jacket. We grabbed an arm apiece and I think I had hold of the left arm.

He was struggling and kicking out and shouting and swearing, but I cannot be more precise as to what he was saying.

I could smell he had been drinking.

He was still trying to get to the other man, who by this time was lying on the ground, his face covered in blood, but we held on. Then the police arrived.

Supportive evidence re exhibit (OAKDEN)

Just after the police took the man in the leather jacket away, I saw Graham pick up a broken bottle. It looked exactly like the broken bottle the man had used in the attack.

I have been shown a broken bottle (GO/1) and can say that it appears identical both to the one used by the man in the attack and the one picked up by Graham.

Opinion WHY

I have no idea why this fight took place, except to suppose it was about someone queue jumping.

Signed ...... W.A. GRIGG   169

**Defences
(disproves
possible
grievance)
(disproves
need for
violence)**

I can definitely say that there had been no queue jumping because I recall that the man in the leather jacket arrived in the queue, just in front of Graham and me. At that time I think the man in the sports jacket was already in the queue, although I cannot be sure.

Having said all that, the attack seemed totally unprovoked and there was no reason that I could see why the man in the leather jacket fought with the other man.   There was certainly no reason to use the bottle.

**Relevant
fact
Conduct of
victim
Further
assists in
disproving
any defence**

I have been asked if I can recall seeing the man in the sports jacket hit the man in the leather jacket. I can say that I do seem to remember him hitting the man in the leather jacket, but this was after he himself had been hit several times, with the bottle. I think he hit the man in the leather jacket, with his fist to his chest. I saw only one blow and it was nothing like the serious assault by the man in the leather jacket.

**Relevant
Facts conduct
of Accused**

I have already said that the man in the leather jacket had been drinking and I got the impression that he was slightly drunk.   He was shouting loudly, smelling strongly of drink and his speech was slightly slurred.

**Opinion as
to drunkeness**

However, he wasn't that drunk, becáuse he quietened down   ****4** very quickly when the police arrived.

**Factual
detail
i/d
offender**

I would describe the man in the leather jacket as being between 20 and 25 years of age, about 6'0" tall, very well built, but not fat. He had longish, but not untidy dark hair and I think he had a moustache. He was wearing blue trousers, which may have been jeans. I cannot make any comment about his accent, except to say I don't think it was local.

I would definitely recognise him again.

Signed .... W.A. GRIGG

Name................ Peter Lloyd DENSHAM

Address...... The Old School House, Sefton Lane, Moor Park, LEEDS, Yorkshire

Occupation.. Doctor...............................   Age..29.yrs.(b.19.2.57)

This statement (consisting of   2   pages each signed by me) is true to the best of my knowledge and belief and I make it knowing that if it is tendered in evidence I shall be liable to prosecution if I have wilfully stated in it anything which I know to be false or do not believe to be true.

Dated the........day of June................. 19.--.   ....

Signed........ P.L. DENSHAM ....

<table>
<tr><td>Relevant facts
Intro. matters
proving
expert</td><td>   I am a doctor of medicine, having studied at
LEEDS University and qualified in 1981. Since that time
I have been resident at LEEDS Royal Infirmary and am
currently the senior casualty officer at that hospital.</td></tr>
<tr><td>Offence
detail
proving
g.b.h.</td><td>   At about 12.15 a.m. on Sunday, 1st June 19--
I saw Terence PATTINSON in the casualty department, where
after examination I noted the following injuries.
          There was a large bruise to the right temple,
and there was swelling, tenderness and discoloration in
the vicinity of the bruise.
          The patient's right cheek was swollen, discoloured
and heavily bruised.
          The left cheek had a number of lacerations, I
counted six in all, which ran from the line of the cheek
bone, downwards for approximately three inches. Three
of the lacerations were minor and not deep, while the
remaining three lacerations were deep and bleeding
profusely. These lacerations required 24 stitches.
          There was a large bruise to the left lower ribs
and in the area of the stomach.
          The whole of the patient's face and head was
tender to the touch. The patient complained of pains
in the head and was in a state of mild shock.</td></tr>
<tr><td>Exhibit
supportive
opinion</td><td>   I have today been shown a broken bottle (GO/1)   **9
and can say that the cuts, I have described, on the face
of Terence PATTINSON, would have been caused by a sharp</td></tr>
</table>

Signed............... P.L. DENSHAM ....

Supportive opinion

instrument, similar to this broken bottle (GO/1).

     In my experience as a casualty officer, I have treated literally hundreds of people with injuries, sustained as a result of attacks where weapons have been used.

Expert supportive opinion

     The marks I saw on Terence Pattinson's face are consistent with the kind of injuries I have seen on other patients who have been attacked with a sharp edged weapon, such as a knife or a broken bottle.

172

Signed .... P.L. DENSHAM ....

STATEMENT FORM

Name .... Martin RICHARDS ....

Address ...... West Yorkshire Constabulary, LEEDS, Yorkshire ....

Occupation .. Detective Constable 55 ....   Age .. Over 21 years ......

This statement (consisting of 1 pages each signed by me) is true to the best of my knowledge and belief and I make it knowing that if it is tendered in evidence I shall be liable to prosecution if I have wilfully stated in it anything which I know to be false or do not believe to be true.

Dated the .. 1st .... day of .... June .... 19--... ....

Signed .. M. RICHARDS   D.C.55 ....

Relevant fact (proving he is specialist)

     I am detective constable currently attached to the Scenes of Crime Department, at LEEDS Police Station.

Offence detail (record of injuries)

     At about 12.20 a.m. on Sunday, 1st June 19-- I attended at the casualty department of LEEDS Royal Infirmary, where I saw a Terence James PATTINSON.

     I then took four photograhs of Mr PATTINSON. Three of those photographs were of injuries to Mr PATTINSON's head and face, while the fourth was of marks to his lower chest and stomach.

     All the photographs were taken before Mr PATTINSON had received treatment.

Exhibit

     I have placed these four photographs in an album (MR/1).

Signed... M. RICHARDS   D.C.55 ....

STATEMENT FORM

Name ....Keith James TURNER...

Address ....West Yorkshire Constabulary, LEEDS, Yorkshire......................

Occupation....Police Constable 965..........   Age .....Over 21 years...

This statement (consisting of 1   pages each signed by me) is true to the best of my knowledge and belief and I make it knowing that if it is tendered in evidence I shall be liable to prosecution if I have wilfully stated in it anything which I know to be false or do not believe to be true.

Dated the...........1st..day of...........June.............................. 19..--.. ....

Signed............. K.J. TURNER   P.C.965 ....

Factual detail 'Time, day, date, place'	At about 11.55 p.m. on Saturday, 31st May 19--, I was on duty at the junction of Scagell Road and Market Walk, LEEDS, with Police Constable 883 ALFORD.
	At that time Constable ALFORD went to a queue of people standing by the Pie and Peas stall. I joined him about two minutes later.
I/D offender	I then saw him with the Accused HURFORD, and I went with Constable ALFORD and HURFORD to a nearby police car.
Supportive evidence (ALFORD)	I was present, at the car, while HURFORD was searched and can state that no weapons or bottles were found on HURFORD.
Admissible hearsay supportive (OAKDEN)	Just after the search had taken place the police car was approached by a member of the public, who said, to Constable ALFORD, in the presence and hearing of the Accused HURFORD, 'Here's the bottle Constable, he must have dropped it, when he saw you'.
Exhibit	That person then handed to Constable ALFORD a broken bottle (GO/1).
Conduct of Accused	HURFORD said, 'Nothing to do with me mate'. I then accompanied Constable ALFORD and HURFORD to LEEDS Police Station.
Supportive evidence (ALFORD)	At 2.30 a.m. on Sunday, 1st June, 19-- I was present in an interview room, when Constable ALFORD interviewed HURFORD, in the present of Mr CHANTER, a
Exhibit	solicitor. I took a contemporaneous note (KT/1) of that interview.

Signed........... K.J. TURNER   P.C.965 ....

174

STATEMENT FORM

Name .... John Gordon ALFORD ....

Address .... West Yorkshire Constabulary, LEEDS, Yorkshire ....

Occupation ... Police Constable 883 ....   Age .... Over 21 years ....

This statement (consisting of   2   pages each signed by me) is true to the best of my knowledge and belief and I make it knowing that if it is tendered in evidence I shall be liable to prosecution if I have wilfully stated in it anything which I know to be false or do not believe to be true.

Dated the .... day of .... 19 .-.-...   ....
         1st   June

Signed .... J.G. ALFORD   P.C.883

Factual detail 'time, day, date, place'	At about 11.55 p.m. on Saturday, 31st May, 19-- I was on duty at the junction of Scagell Road and Market Walk, LEEDS, with Police Constable 965 TURNER. At that time I went to a queue of people standing by the Pie and Peas stall. Constable TURNER said, 'Looks like a big crowd in the Crypt tonight. We'd better see the place out.'
I/D offender	I there saw the Accused HURFORD, being held by two men. One of the men, I later learned to be a
Admissible hearsay/ supportive (OAKDEN)	Mr Graham OAKDEN said, in the presence and hearing of the Accused, 'This man has just attacked that man, with a bottle'. He pointed to a man lying on the ground, with an injury to his head. OAKDEN went on, 'It looked a totally senseless thing to do'.
Relevant facts Conduct of Accused	I said to HURFORD, 'I am arresting you on suspicion of causing grievous bodily harm'. I cautioned him and he said, 'It was self-defence Constable, just self-defence'. I said to HURFORD, 'Where's the bottle?' HURFORD said, 'Bottle, what bottle? I didn't have any bottle'. I then took HURFORD to the police car, where he was searched and placed in the rear of the vehicle. I found no bottle in HURFORD's possession.

Signed .... J.G. ALFORD   P.C.883

175

Admissible hearsay supportive (OAKDEN)

At that time Mr OAKDEN approached the vehicle and said, in the presence and hearing of the Accused, 'Here's the bottle Constable, he must have dropped it when he saw you'. Mr OAKDEN then handed to me a broken

Exhibit

bottle (GO/1).

Conduct of Accused

HURFORD said, 'Nothing to do with me mate'.

I then took HURFORD to LEEDS Police Station.

Offence detail (admission)

At 2.30 a.m. on Sunday, 1st June 19-- I again saw HURFORD in the presence of his solicitor, Mr CHANTER, in an interview room at the Police Station.

Exhibit

Also present was Constable TURNER, who took a contemporaneous note (KT/1) of that interview.

Relevant fact

At 5.45 a.m. that same morning I formally charged HURFORD with the offence of causing grievous bodily harm to Terence PATTINSON, cautioned him and he said, 'I understand'.

176   Signed .... J.G. ALFORD   P.C.883

INTERVIEW RECORD FORM

INTERVIEW OF .... Malcolm Phillip HURFORD ....

ADDRESS .... 101 Egremont Terrace, LEEDS, Yorkshire ....

Occupation ..... Labourer .... Date of Birth ... 14.4.64 ....

Interviewing Officers ..... P.C.883 ALFORD ....
.... P.C.965 TURNER ....
......................................,.................................

Other persons present ...... Mr CHANTER, solicitor for HURFORD ....
....

Date of Interview .... 1.6.-- .... Place of Interview ..... LEEDS Police Station

Time commenced .... 0230 hrs .... Time concluded .... 0340 hrs ....

	P.C. ALFORD	'Earlier on this evening I arrested you, near the Pie and Peas stall, in Scagell Road, LEEDS. That was in connection with an allegation that you had caused grievous bodily harm to another person. I now intend to ask you a number of questions in connection with that matter.' CAUTIONED.
Caution	P.C. ALFORD	'Do you understand?'
	HURFORD	'Yes.'
Factual detail 'Time, day, date, place'	P.C. ALFORD	'Where were you at about 11.45 p.m. to 11.50 p.m. on the evening of Saturday, 31st May 19--?'
	HURFORD	'You mean last evening. You know where I was, I was waiting to get some grub at the Pie and Peas stall. You know I was there.'
	P.C. ALFORD	'I arrested you at about 11.55 p.m. I am asking you now, where you were about ten minutes before that.'
	HURFORD	'I'd been in the queue about five minutes or so before you came along.'
Factual detail — actual location	P.C. ALFORD	'In the queue, were you standing behind a young man, who was wearing a sports jacket?'
	HURFORD	'I don't know if it is the same one you are on about, but I was behind a young bloke with a jacket on, yes.'
Additional allegation	P.C. ALFORD	'Did you have some conversation with this man?'
	HURFORD	'I don't think so.'

(*Signed*) .... M.P. HURFORD ....
                         J. CHANTER

177

INTERVIEW OF   Malcolm Phillip HURFORD   **Continuation Sheet.**

	P.C. ALFORD	'Did you talk to anyone while you were standing in the queue?'
	HURFORD	'I can't remember.'
Additional allegations	P.C. ALFORD	'Do you recall two men standing behind you, **18 who later grabbed hold of you?'
	HURFORD	'I know two blokes grabbed hold of me yes, but I don't know where they were standing before they took hold of me.'
and	P.C. ALFORD	'Those two men describe being behind you in the queue and seeing and hearing you have a discussion with the young man in the sports jacket. What do you say?'
relevant facts	HURFORD	'I don't remember that.'
	P.C. ALFORD	'The way they describe this conversation, you were having a disagreement with this young man. Would this be right?'
Conduct of Accused	HURFORD	'Now I know who you're on about. Yes, he'd pushed in front of me and I told him he was out of order.'
	P.C. ALFORD	'Was there much discussion between the two of you?'
	HURFORD	'I was a bit upset because he'd pushed in front, that's all.'
	P.C. ALFORD	'What did you say can you remember?'
	HURFORD	'No, I can't.'
	P.C. ALFORD	'It is alleged you were swearing and shouting, were you?'
	HURFORD	'I can't remember that.'
	P.C. ALFORD	'It is alleged you said, "You're jumping the queue, mate, get back where you belong". Do you recall that?'
	HURFORD	'I think I did say that, yes.'
	P.C. ALFORD	'What did the young man say?'
	HURFORD	'He told me to piss off.'

(*Signed*) ....
                    M.P. HURFORD
                    J. CHANTER

INTERVIEW OF   Malcolm Phillip HURFORD   **Continuation Sheet.**

	P.C. ALFORD	'That is not what the young man says. Neither do the two men who were behind you. They all say that the young man quietly and calmly told you that you were mistaken. What do you say?'
	HURFORD	'They're liars.'
	P.C. ALFORD	'It is then alleged, when the young man pointed out to you that he hadn't jumped the queue, you said, "You bloody well have you shit, I won't tell you again, bugger off to the back." Is that right?'
Additional allegations	HURFORD	'I don't remember saying that.'
	P.C. ALFORD	'It is then alleged that the young man turned around to the front and you shouted to him, "Don't turn your back on me, mate".'
	HURFORD	'I don't remember that.'
Offence detail 'assault'	P.C. ALFORD	'It is then alleged that you took an empty beer bottle from your pocket, did you?'
	HURFORD	'No.'
	P.C. ALFORD	'The young man then alleges you shouted at him, "Right, you've asked for it". Did you?'
	HURFORD	'I don't remember that.'
	P.C. ALFORD	'It is then alleged that you lunged at the young man and struck him several blows, using the bottle as a weapon. Did you?'
	HURFORD	'No I didn't do that. I didn't have any bottle did I?'
	P.C. ALFORD	'The bottle is alleged to have smashed during one of the blows, but it is alleged you continued to use the broken bottle as a weapon. Did you?'
Exhibit	HURFORD	'No.'
	P.C. ALFORD	'This is the broken bottle that was allegedly used by you, in this attack (indicated GO/1). Did you use this?'

(*Signed*) ....
                    M.P. HURFORD
                    J. CHANTER

179

INTERVIEW OF   Malcolm Phillip HURFORD   **Continuation Sheet.**

	HURFORD	'I've told you I never had any bottle in the first place.'
Supportive evidence proving conduct	P.C. ALFORD	'I must tell you that the two men who were standing behind you, have both told the police that they witnessed this attack. First of all they confirm that you were swearing and shouting in the manner I have described. What do you say?'
	HURFORD	'They're liars.'
	P.C. ALFORD	'Both of them also say that they saw you take this bottle (indicating GO/1) from your pocket. What do you say?'
	HURFORD	'I've never seen that before in my life.'
	P.C. ALFORD	'Both men then go on to describe seeing you using the bottle in the attack upon the young man.'
Supportive evidence proving assault — Offence detail and possession of weapon	HURFORD	'They're wrong.'
	P.C. ALFORD	'One of the men goes further. He states that you were still holding this bottle when they went and grabbed hold of you, but that you then dropped it. That man, Mr OAKDEN, searched in the area and found this broken bottle (GO/1) and states that it is the one you were using in the assault. In other words he is positively identifying you as the assailant and this as the weapon you used.'
Offence detail admission	HURFORD	'All right, all right, there's no need to go on. I went a bit over the top that's all.'
	P.C. ALFORD	'Are you now admitting that you were the person who attacked the young man in the sports jacket?' **19
	HURFORD	'Yes, it was me, you know it was, there's no point in arguing about it anymore.'
Proving exhibit	P.C. ALFORD	'Did you use this bottle (indicating (GO/1) in the course of that attack?'
	HURFORD	'Yes I did. I don't know what got into me. I could have sworn he jumped the queue and that was the start of it.'

(*Signed*) ....
M.P. HURFORD
J. CHANTER

180

INTERVIEW OF   Malcolm Phillip HURFORD   **Continuation Sheet.**

	P.C. ALFORD	'You are surely not saying that jumping a queue is an excuse for this kind of assault are you?'
	HURFORD	'No I'm not. I've said I went over the top.'
Specific actions by defendant confirmed	P.C. ALFORD	'Can you remember where you hit the young man, with this bottle?.
	HURFORD	'I think I hit him once on the shoulder.'
	P.C. ALFORD	'How many times did you hit him?'
	HURFORD	'Two or three times.'
	P.C. ALFORD	'Where?'
	HURFORD	'I was aiming for the shoulders and arms, but I may have hit him by accident on the head.'
	P.C. ALFORD	'It is alleged that all the blows were to the head.'
	HURFORD	'That can't be right because I hit him in the chest or stomach.'
	P.C. ALFORD	'With the bottle?'
	HURFORD	'No, with my knee.'
	P.C. ALFORD	'Fair enough, but all the blows to the head were said to be deliberate.'
	HURFORD	'I can't say anymore on that.'
	P.C. ALFORD	'Do you remember the bottle breaking?'
	HURFORD	'I remember it did break, yes.'
	P.C. ALFORD	'How?'
	HURFORD	'I don't remember.'
	P.C. ALFORD	'It is alleged it broke as a result of one of the blows you struck to the young man's head.'
Offence detail	HURFORD	'It could have.'
	P.C. ALFORD	'What happened then?'
	HURFORD	'What do you mean?'
	P.C. ALFORD	'Did you carry on using the bottle as a weapon?'
	HURFORD	'Not intentionally. I didn't realise it had broken until I'd used it a couple of times. Then I stopped.'

                                                    M. P. HURFORD
           (*Signed*) ....
                                     J. CHANTER   181

INTERVIEW OF   Malcolm Phillip HURFORD   **Continuation Sheet.**

g.b.h.	P.C. ALFORD	'It is alleged you deliberately pushed the broken bottle into the face of the young man. Did you?'
	HURFORD	'I meant to hit him, but not with the broken bottle, it just happened.'
	P.C. ALFORD	'The young man you hit has sustained a number of cuts to his face, caused by this bottle. Those cuts have required 24 stitches. Those are serious injuries.
	HURFORD	'I didn't mean to do that.'
	P.C. ALFORD	'What did you mean to do?' **∗∗20**
	HURFORD	'I don't know. I just thought he'd jumped in front of me and it went on from there.'
	P.C. ALFORD	'It is alleged that after striking the young man a number of blows to the face and head with this bottle, you then kicked him in the groin or stomach area. Did you?'
	HURFORD	'I've already said I did that.'
Relevant facts	P.C. ALFORD	'It is alleged that the young man then fell to the ground. Did he?'
	HURFORD	'Yes, he did'
Conduct of Accused after offence	P.C. ALFORD	'It is alleged you then continued to try to assault him further, with the broken bottle. Did you?'
	HURFORD	'I don't remember that.'
	P.C. ALFORD	'The two men I have already told you about, say that if they hadn't moved in and restrained you right away, you would have continued to attack the young man. What do you say?'
	HURFORD	'It was over by the time they got hold of me.'
	P.C. ALFORD	'They both say that you shouted at them, "Leave go of me, I'll kill the bastard". Did you say those things?'
	HURFORD	'I don't think so.'

(*Signed*) .... M.P. HURFORD ....

J. CHANTER

182

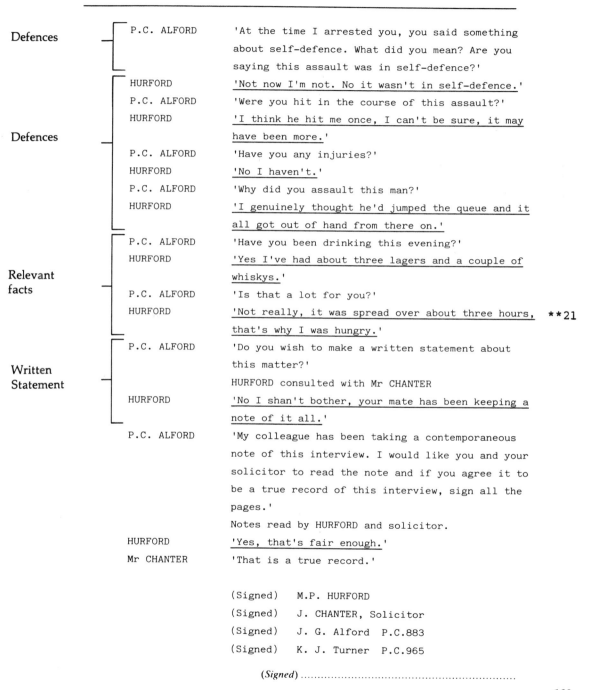

INTERVIEW OF   Malcolm Phillip HURFORD   **Continuation Sheet.**

Defences	P.C. ALFORD	'At the time I arrested you, you said something about self-defence. What did you mean? Are you saying this assault was in self-defence?'
	HURFORD	'Not now I'm not. No it wasn't in self-defence.'
	P.C. ALFORD	'Were you hit in the course of this assault?'
Defences	HURFORD	'I think he hit me once, I can't be sure, it may have been more.'
	P.C. ALFORD	'Have you any injuries?'
	HURFORD	'No I haven't.'
	P.C. ALFORD	'Why did you assault this man?'
	HURFORD	'I genuinely thought he'd jumped the queue and it all got out of hand from there on.'
Relevant facts	P.C. ALFORD	'Have you been drinking this evening?'
	HURFORD	'Yes I've had about three lagers and a couple of whiskys.'
	P.C. ALFORD	'Is that a lot for you?'
	HURFORD	'Not really, it was spread over about three hours, **21 that's why I was hungry.'
Written Statement	P.C. ALFORD	'Do you wish to make a written statement about this matter?'
		HURFORD consulted with Mr CHANTER
	HURFORD	'No I shan't bother, your mate has been keeping a note of it all.'
	P.C. ALFORD	'My colleague has been taking a contemporaneous note of this interview. I would like you and your solicitor to read the note and if you agree it to be a true record of this interview, sign all the pages.'
		Notes read by HURFORD and solicitor.
	HURFORD	'Yes, that's fair enough.'
	Mr CHANTER	'That is a true record.'

(Signed)   M.P. HURFORD
(Signed)   J. CHANTER, Solicitor
(Signed)   J. G. Alford P.C.883
(Signed)   K. J. Turner P.C.965

(Signed) ....

COLLATOR

Date		Information	
9.9.--		Leeds Mags. Court. A.B.H. 6 months' impt. sus. 12 months. Offen. weapon 6 months' impt. sus. 12 months conc. M.O. Assaulted visiting football fans, using a beer bottle, during course of attack.	

```
SURNAME          :   HURFORD
FORENAMES        :   MALCOLM
                 :   PHILLIP

OPERATOR         :   QRFSUP

URN              :   048643
```

```
CONVICTIONS        1

   1  9-SEP-19---  COURT   :   LEEDS
                   TYPE    :   MAGISTRATES COURT

            1.   OFF.  :   ASSAULT OCCASIONING ACTUAL BODILY HARM
                 SENT. :   6 MTHS IMPRISONMENT SUSPENDED 12 MONTHS

            2.   OFF.  :   OFFENSIVE WEAPON
                 SENT. :   6 MTHS IMPRISONMENT CONCURRENT SUSPENDED
                           12 MONTHS
```

```
NNNN

Call duration: 00:00:32     Packets out: 0     Packets in: 433
*** Cleared -- 0000
```

Accident in the street: occurrence statements; occurrence report; foreign station enquiry report

STATEMENT FORM

Name .... Edwin JOHNS

Address .... 2 Back Road West, ST IVES, Cornwall

Occupation .... Building contractor ....   Age 55 yrs (b.19.4.28)

This statement (consisting of 2 pages each signed by me) is true to the best of my knowledge and belief and I make it knowing that if it is tendered in evidence I shall be liable to prosecution if I have wilfully stated in it anything which I know to be false or do not believe to be true.

Dated the... 1st ....day of.. July .... 19.--...   ....

Signed. E. JOHNS ....

       I am a building contractor and have in my employ 14 men. Three of my men have been working on a shop front at CURNOWS' gift shop, in Fore Street, ST IVES, for the past two weeks. The work entails resurfacing the wall and repairing and replacing some tiles on the roof. In order to facilitate this work we have erected scaffolding 30' high, on the shop front. However, due to the narrowness of the street, we have been unable to erect a lift, so all the materials and waste have to be carried up and down by hand.

       In addition to myself **the** three men working on the site have been James COLLINS of 2 Coastguard Cottages, William PERKINS of 3 Digey Cottages, The Stennack and Colin PENBERTHY (b.1.1.61) of 3 Carrick Way, The Headland. All the men come from ST IVES.

       Since we have been working on the shop front, I have had to speak to both William PERKINS and Colin PENBERTHY and instruct them both not to carry too much, when they are going up and down the scaffolding. As I have said, the street is narrow, it is the peak of the summer season and so I have told them both to be extra careful and carry small amounts only.

       Yesterday, that is Thursday, 30th June 19-- I had to speak to Colin because I found that he was bringing down something like two dozen slates in one go. I had already told him that 10 or 12 was a safe number.

       Colin apologised and said he was only trying to speed things up.

Signed... E. JOHNS ....

I said to him, 'Never mind about speeding things up, you just do what you're told'.

Colin said he would and that was the end of the matter.

Today, Friday, 1st July 19-- I came to the site and worked with the men for the early part of the morning. Again Colin and William were removing slates from the roof.

At about 12.10 p.m. to 12.15 p.m. I left to go to the bank and returned about 15 minutes later.

Just as I arrived I saw William and James running over to Colin who was lying on the ground. He had just fallen off the scaffolding.

I could see near him a pile of broken tiles. I later made a rough tally of the tiles and although I cannot be precise, due to damage, I estimated that there were something like 20 tiles in the pile at least.

If Colin was carrying that number, before he fell, then he was carrying too many in my opinion and it was certainly contrary to what I had told him to do.

When I arrived back from the bank, I could see Colin was badly hurt. He was unconscious and bleeding from the head.

I don't think anyone actually witnessed Colin falling, although James told me that a woman holiday maker, who had been talking to Colin, may have seen him on the scaffolding, just before he fell.

I was present when the ambulance arrived and took Colin to the Edward HAIN hospital, in ST IVES, where on admission, Colin was still found to be unconscious.

                        Signed ....E. JOHNS........................

STATEMENT FORM

Name ..... William PERKINS

Address ..... No. 3 Digey Cottages, The Stennack, ST IVES, Cornwall

Occupation ..... Labourer ..... Age ..... 33 yrs (b.21.8.51)

This statement (consisting of 2 pages each signed by me) is true to the best of my knowledge and belief and I make it knowing that if it is tendered in evidence I shall be liable to prosecution if I have wilfully stated in it anything which I know to be false or do not believe to be true.

Dated the ..... 1st ..... day of ..... JULY ..... 19.--. .....

Signed ..... W. PERKINS .....

I am a labourer, and I am employed by Edwin JOHNS, building contractor, of Back Road West, ST IVES, Cornwall.

Recently, during the past two weeks, we have been working on the wall of CURNOWS' gift shop, in Fore Street, ST IVES.

Also working on the site have been Colin PENBERTHY, from 3 Carrick Way, The Headland, ST IVES, James COLLINS of 2 Coastguard Cottages, ST IVES and Mr Edwin JOHNS, himself.

Because the work has involved repairs to the top part of the wall, some of the slates on the roof have had to be changed and, during Thursday, 30th June 19-- and the morning of Friday, 1st July 19--, Colin PENBERTHY and I have been removing the slates from the roof.

In order to get to the roof we have erected scaffolding outside CURNOWS' and have been using that to get to the roof.

Yesterday (30.6.--), during the afternoon, Mr JOHNS had words with Colin and told him that he was trying to carry too many slates, down from the roof, in one go. There is no lift so we have to carry the slates down by hand. Generally speaking 10 or 12 slates is about the limit, but I do know Colin has tried to carry double that number.

This morning, 1st July 19--, we were all working on the wall again and during the early part of the morning Mr JOHNS was on the site and Colin was bringing down about 10 or 12 slates at a time.

Signed ..... W. PERKINS .....

We had a break for a couple of hours during the morning, when we went to get some more equipment, then at about 12.15 p.m. started on the roof again. Colin and I were going up and down the scaffolding and James was mixing the concrete. Mr JOHNS had slipped away for a few minutes.

On his second trip down Colin had about two dozen tiles in his hands and I said to him, 'That's a bit dodgy, carrying all that weight'.

He said, 'No problem, I can manage it easy, we'll finish quicker, this way'.

Then he went up for a third time.

I was on the ground stacking the tiles, and giving James a hand with the gear, when I heard a woman shout out, 'That man's going to fall' or words to that effect.

I looked around and saw Colin, on the scaffolding with a load of slates in his hands. I could see there were something like 20 or more. He was obviously having trouble holding on to the slates, so I shouted, 'Drop the damn slates', but then he fell from the scaffolding, onto the ground.

I only saw Colin, just before he fell and he must have just stepped off the ladder, from the roof, to the first level on the scaffolding, when he fell. There was no one else on the scaffolding.

The weather for the past week, including today, has been fine and dry and the scaffolding and platforms on the scaffolding are dry and in no way slippery.

I think Colin was trying to carry too many slates and overbalanced. It was an accident.

190

STATEMENT FORM

Name .... James COLLINS ....

Address .... 2 Coastguard Cottages, ST IVES, Cornwall ....

Occupation... Labourer ....   Age ... 35 yrs. (b.16.8.49)

This statement (consisting of 2   pages each signed by me) is true to the best of my knowledge and belief and I make it knowing that if it is tendered in evidence I shall be liable to prosecution if I have wilfully stated in it anything which I know to be false or do not believe to be true.

Dated the .... 1st .... day of .... July .... 19.--..   ....

Signed .... J. COLLINS ....

I am a labourer working for Edwin JOHNS, building contractor of Back Road West, ST IVES, Cornwall.

For the past two weeks, I have been working on the shop front of CURNOWS' Gift Shop, in Fore Street, ST IVES, with Colin PENBERTHY of 3 Carrick Way, The Headland, ST IVES, William PERKINS of 3 Digey Cottages, ST IVES, and Edwin JOHNS.

In addition to facing up the wall, we have had to remove some of the slates from the roof and in order to do that we have put up scaffolding.

My job has been on the ground, mixing and carrying, while Colin and William have been up on the scaffolding, bringing down the tiles.

On the morning of Friday, 1st July 19-- we had been working on the site and Mr JOHNS, who had been there most of the morning, left to go to the bank, at about 12.10 p.m.

A few minutes later a number of holiday makers stood watching us and when Colin came down, with a load of tiles, he spoke to a woman, who was standing there, who I think was from the North of England.

I remember her saying to Colin words to the effect that it looked dangerous work, carrying all those tiles down the scaffolding. Colin said something like, 'I usually carry 20 or 30, it's easy when you're used to it' and he laughed.

Then he said, 'You watch, it's easy when you know how', and then he went up the scaffolding.

Signed .... J. COLLINS ....

191

The woman wandered off across the road and joined her husband, near the <u>Castle</u> public house, and the next I heard was the same woman shout, 'Look he's going to fall' or words to that effect.

I looked up, just in time to see Colin falling from the scaffolding, with a load of slates in his hands.

He landed on the roadway on his shoulder and I could see straight away it was a bad fall.

I went across to where he was and could see he was unconscious and pale. He was bleeding from the head. Near where he was there was a pile of broken slates that looked like about 18 or 20, I would estimate, though I did not count them. Most of them were broken.

The same woman, who had spoken to Colin earlier, came across and then dashed off saying she was going to telephone for the ambulance.

I stayed looking after Colin until the ambulance arrived.

It looks as though this accident happened because Colin lost his balance on the scaffolding. It may have been due to his trying to carry too many tiles. I can't say for sure of course, because I wasn't watching him before he fell, but I think the woman who spoke to him earlier, was watching, but I can't be sure.

There was no one else on the scaffolding when Colin fell. William was on the ground with me and Mr JOHNS only returned to the scene, just as Colin fell.

                     Signed .... J. COLLINS ....

OCCURRENCE REPORT

...ST. IVES............. Station

....'A'.................. Division

...Western.............. Area   ....2nd. July................... 19.--....

Subject ......Colin PENBERTHY (b.1.1.61) of 3 Carrick Way, The Headland, ST IVES
....

...............................Industrial Accident................................
....

Officer Reporting ....Constable.No...161.......D.J..BRAY..........................

To ....Ch/SUPT..J..ALLEN...........   ....'A'........................... Division

---

Sir,

A brief introduction

This report concerns an industrial accident, which occurred at about 12.30 p.m. on Friday, 1st July 19--, in Fore Street, ST IVES, when Colin PENBERTHY, fell from scaffolding, onto the ground and received serious injuries. Briefly the facts are as follows:

A precis of the evidence

During the past two weeks, Mr Edwin JOHNS, building contractor of No. 2 Back Road West, ST IVES, has been carrying out repair work to the front and roof of CURNOWS' Gift shop, Fore Street, ST IVES.

Three of his workmen, including PENBERTHY, have been employed on that work and, in order to carry out such work, scaffolding has had to be erected outside the shop, to a height of some 30 feet. All materials and waste have had to be carried by hand, and this includes the removal of a large number of tiles from the roof.

Mr JOHNS has warned his men not to attempt to carry too much, when conveying materials and had to remind PENBERTHY of this precaution, as recently as Thursday, 30th June 19--.

At about 12.10 p.m. on Friday, 1st July 19--, JOHNS left the site and upon his return, some 15 or 20 minutes later, found that PENBERTHY had fallen off the scaffolding, while carrying a load of slates.

The two other men working at the site, both tell of PENBERTHY attempting to carry more than was thought to be safe.

193

A
precis
of
the
evidence

William PERKINS, a labourer of 3 Digey Cottages, The Stennack, ST IVES confirms that JOHNS gave advice concerning safety and states that just before the accident PENBERTHY told him (PERKINS) of his intention to carry more than the suggested number of tiles.

James COLLINS, a labourer of 2 Coastguard Cottages, ST IVES also confirms that immediately prior to the accident PENBERTHY stated his intention to carry a large number of tiles. COLLINS further tells of a conversation PENBERTHY had with a female holiday maker in which he (PENBERTHY) boasted about how easy it was to carry such loads.

Mr Phillip HARDCASTLE, a holiday maker, of No. 50 Otley Road, LEEDS, Yorkshire describes having his attention drawn to the accident by his wife Angela. Mr HARDCASTLE actually saw PENBERTHY fall and can say that, at the time, he (PENBERTHY) was attempting to carry a load of slates.

Other
matters

PENBERTHY was taken to the Edward HAIN Hospital, at ST IVES where an X-ray examination, on admission, revealed that he had fractured his skull.

PENBERTHY remains stable, though unconscious and his condition is described as critical. It is too early, at this stage, for medical experts to fully diagnose PENBERTHY's condition, accordingly a statement, as yet, has not been obtained from the hospital staff.

This report is submitted for your information to be retained for use by the Coroner, if required.

Constable 161

FOREIGN STATION ENQUIRY REPORTS

ST IVES .... Station

'A' .... Division

Western .... Area   7th July 19.--

Subject .... PENBERTHY .... Accident in the street

Officer Reporting .. Constable No. 161 .. D.J. BRAY

To .... Ch/Supt J. ALLEN .... 'A' .... Division

Sir,

A brief introduction

This report concerns a request for further police enquiries in connection with an industrial accident which occurred in Fore Street, ST IVES when a local man, Colin PENBERTHY, fell from scaffolding onto the ground and received injuries.

PENBERTHY has failed to regain consciousness and is currently on the critical list.

A precis of the evidence

A number of persons witnessed this accident, including a Mr Phillip HARDCASTLE, of 50 Otley Road, LEEDS, Yorkshire, who was on holiday in ST IVES, at the time, but has since returned to LEEDS.

He was accompanied by his wife Angela, who, it is thought, witnessed this accident, and more importantly, the events leading up to it.

James COLLINS, another witness at the scene, describes the injured man, talking to a female holiday maker, thought to be Mrs HARDCASTLE.

The statements of COLLINS and HARDCASTLE are attached.

Other matters

I ask that an officer interview Mrs HARDCASTLE in connection with this incident and take a statement from her and that the following points, in particular, be covered in that statement.

(a) Was she the woman to whom PENBERTHY spoke, as described in the statement from COLLINS?

(b) If so, what did PENBERTHY say to her?

Other matters

(c) Can she give any estimate of the number of tiles being carried by PENBERTHY immediately before his fall?

I ask that this report and the attached statements be forwarded to the Chief Officer of Police, West Yorkshire Constabulary, LEEDS, Yorkshire, in order that an officer may carry out this enquiry.

Constable No. 161

Index